SCENES

for ACTORS AND VOICES

by Daws Butler

SCENES

for ACTORS AND VOICES

by Daws Butler

Edited by

Ben Ohmart

and

Joe Bevilacqua

BearManor Media
2003

For information, address:

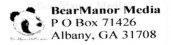

BearManor Media
P O Box 71426
Albany, GA 31708

bearmanormedia.com

Cover design by Lorie B. Kellogg
Typesetting and layout by John Teehan

Published in the USA by BearManor Media
ISBN—0-9714570-6-9
Library of Congress Control No. 2003100760

The official Daws Butler site can be found at

http://www.dawsbutler.com

TABLE OF CONTENTS

SO YOU WANT TO BE
A VOICE ACTOR...

Do you love "doing voices" more than anything else in the world? Is your voice your favorite 'plaything'? Are you willing to dedicate your *entire life* to it; forsaking the "normal" human pursuits such as stable personal relationships and social activities, along with planned vacations and "regular" working hours with predictable pay? Are you willing to spend an unreasonable amount of your money to live in the quagmire of chaos known as Los Angeles, spending the better part of your days stuck in a car, attempting to deal with the most infuriating traffic conditions imaginable? Do you have an "open mind"—meaning that you can be comfortable with all kinds of people and human behavior, unrestricted by rigid or fundamentalist beliefs and prejudices?

If not, then *LOOK NO FURTHER! Voice acting is NOT for You*—other than as a delightful hobby to entertain yourself and friends, with perhaps an occasional 'public display' of your talents (such as recordings for small theater productions, answering machines, or schools and churches and the like). Otherwise, just keep on being a loyal fan—we all cherish the knowledge that our work is not only enjoyed, but actually appreciated by folks who know the difference, and understand a little of what goes into the business of "making funny voices."

...If you are indeed serious about it, here's what you'll need:

1) **A good "ear."** If you're able to distinguish—not just different voices—but all kinds of dialects, along with the specific vocal qualities and layers of subtlety that make up good (or not-so-good) character voices.

2) A great **sense of humor** and a deep appreciation of actors and other performers.

3) A real **love and respect for words**, the intelligence to use them impressively, and of course the **reading skills** that would naturally apply.

4) A **passion for performing** with "wild abandon" in front of a microphone in a confined space, without the benefit of a live audience—and the **good manners** to graciously accept the scrutiny of "fussy" directors.

1

5) An "iron clad" sense of **self-confidence**, tempered with a fair amount of **patience**, plus a good deal of emotional and physical **stamina**, enabling you to plunge forward against all odds into the brutally discouraging world of show business. A little bit of **"business sense"** wouldn't hurt either.

6) A reliable means of **transportation** and Thomas Bros. Map Book of Los Angeles (and/or access to MapQuest via computer and printer); your own **phone line with fax and answering machine** (a cell phone comes in handy as well); plus some "better than average" **sound recording gear**, along with a good working knowledge of audio & video devices.

..and Last—but surprisingly—Least important:

7) **A "good" voice**. You don't really need to have an amazing sounding voice to accomplish good character voice work. What's really important is the *Acting*. Techniques to stretch your range and focus or enhance your own natural vocal qualities may be developed along the way. A truly great or distinctive voice is only a big advantage if you intend to make a living announcing or singing, but is only an asset for a voice *actor* if you want to specialize in narration and straight commercial 'Voice Overs.'

Eventually you will need to make **connections** in show business, create a good **Demo** recording of your vocal talents, join our **Union**(s): S.A.G./A.F.T.R.A., and get an **Agent**—*all of which* are *a lot harder* than they sound.

D. BUTLER DID IT

*A Rambling Diatribe About Getting to Know an Amazing Man
and The Daws Butler Workshop Experience*

How can I best describe what The Man and his Workshop were really like? As I thought back upon my own experience, it began to take the form of a "Real Life Adventure" story. Daws Butler always chided himself for being "verbose"… And having been so greatly influenced by him, I'm afraid my storytelling may also be a bit more "ornate" than necessary; but since this is in tribute to him, I figure I might as well let the words tumble out freely in this somewhat elaborate personal account of my journey into the World of Voice Acting. The quotes, incidentally, are taken strictly from my own foggy memories, and I'm only presuming what was actually said, embellished through my familiarity with these people. (There were, naturally, no real notes or transcripts taken at the time.)

MEETING A MASTER

Ah. Daws Butler. I sure knew that name—as the legendary genius behind the voices of all those great Hanna/Barbera Cartoon Stars. I had imagined him to be a tall, imposing, somber gentleman; something like a balding Basil Rathbone-type, in a formal "smoking jacket"—complete with monogrammed pocket—gesturing eloquently with a smoldering Meerschaum pipe while mulling over a script. "He's a lovely man. I'm sure he won't mind you coming to watch us work. You've got nothing to worry about at all. Daws is very easy to talk to." The reassuring voice over the phone was none other than June Foray (best known as Rocky the Flying Squirrel), in the momentous conversation that preceded our first 'in-person' meeting.

My uncle Burt, you see, had become casually acquainted with June, knowing her as one of his "regulars" at the neighborhood store where he worked. I was flabbergasted one day when I excitedly blurted out that name (having suddenly spotted it in the credits of the "Bullwinkle Show"), and he remarked, "June? She's one of my favorite customers—a real delight to talk to. I'll be damned… I remember her telling me she does all kinds of voices, but I never thought about it much. I see her all the time."

Upon expressing my burning desire to meet the preeminent voice actress and the remarkable "Voice Men" I idolized, Uncle Burt was able to get her O.K. for his 'eccentric 15 year old nephew' to call her, and hopefully arrange a meeting. She was going to be recording a series of voice-over "blackouts" for an experimental local TV show called "The We'll Get You To Bed By Midnight Theatre," in which they presented old movies along with funny banter going in and out of commercials, supplied by a virtual middle-aged married couple, represented by their two pairs of feet in slippers at the foot of their bed in front of their 19 inch TV. You with me so far?

When I entered the soundstage at KTLA in Hollywood, accompanied by my best pal John (still best pals, and currently webmaster of coreyburton.com) my scanning gaze was unable to detect the two figures known to be "Giants of the Industry"—expecting to easily spot the substantial bodies which undoubtedly housed that powerful panoply of character voices. "So you finally made it!" the unmistakable sound of June Foray rang out from an attractive, yet strikingly compact lady standing in the midst of a makeshift arrangement of props and equipment which passed for the modest production's set. Exchanging greetings with this remarkable pixie, we hardly even noticed the plainly attired ordinary looking little man with a healthy crop of graying hair standing next to her, until she proudly introduced him. "And this is Daws Butler!" she cheerfully indicated. Much to my shock, my meager 5'6" frame fairly towered over these two diminutive powerhouses of vocal excellence, who were now placed comfortably down to earth from the cartoon image of an actual pedestal they stood upon in my teenage mind. In what I now know to be his customary fashion, he extended a welcoming hand, with the phrase: "Glad to know you." That quaint expression from a more genteel era would prove to be more telling than I had suspected.

Disarmingly friendly and polite, with an easy smile and playfully animated eyes, the sage and entirely human 'Elf' proceeded to chat up a storm of thoughtful and fascinating conversation all about his experiences in "The Business" and a variety of interesting subjects. We were struck by the sparkling, percussive resonance of his magical voice—it was like being pelted by a musical cascade of marbles launched from that barrel chest, clearly revealing the presence of all those amazing characters simultaneously, blending into one harmonious vibration. The air surrounding him seemed to crackle with electricity, as he freely offered his instructive "play-by-play" narrative throughout the surreal and extraordinary day.

Flashing forward in time, upon June's insistence that I become (much to my reluctance) "pen pals" with a fan of hers from the far flung land of Australia, I had become well acquainted with Keith Scott—who, upon winning a *Sydney TV Guide* contest (testing his now highly sought-after knowledge of Hollywood trivia), was awarded with a free trip to "Tinseltown," complete with accommodations at the Hollywood Holiday Inn. (Keith has since become his nation's leading show business historian/cartoon authority, as well as a successful stand-up comic/impressionist /voice actor, and author of "The Moose that Roared") This sweepstakes prize afforded both of us the perfect excuse to spend a little time in the company of June Foray and Daws Butler at their respective homes, and included a fateful "rap session" (as he labeled the reel of tape) in the impressive little studio Daws kept in his converted Beverly Hills garage.

During our "rap,", the veteran Voice Man was curious to see if our interest in voice acting was more than a passing phase, and had us read and ad-lib a little in front of his magnificent RCA 44 ribbon microphone. We ran through our lists of favorite impressions and vocal tricks we'd been working on, among them, my rudimentary impersonation of Hans Conried. Several months later, having remembered I could simulate that voice, Daws informed me of an opportunity to audition for the Conried-inspired role of "Professor Plumbutter" (in a Disney Educational Media slide-film for schools), as the celebrated actor himself was "back East" touring in the play "The Student Prince" (and wouldn't be available at the time the recording was scheduled for). This would turn out to be my first professional job in show business. With the occasional "What are you working on" call, I continued to keep in touch with the authoritative Mr. Butler.

Well, as we all know, one thing leads to another, and I started to 'grow roots' with the Disney company, being called in to read for another Conried role the following year; but my career didn't exactly "catch fire," and losing interest in the lackluster Radio/TV/ Film courses I briefly attended at CSUN, found myself behind the counter at the local Radio Shack store. Between handing out "Battery of the Month Club" cards and ringing up the smattering of minor sales one evening, my mom called up the store to let me know that Daws Butler was trying to reach me, with some exciting news. With customer activity slowed down to a closing time trickle, I immediately returned the call to the now familiar, highly esteemed Mentor.

AS I RECALL:
...IT ALL STARTED...

"Hello?" Over the telephone he always sounded so young, I was never completely sure if it was really him at first. "Izziss Daws Butler?" I asked tentatively. "Speaking..." he replied. Maybe another chance to audition, I secretly hoped. "You...wanted to talk to me about something?" It took a moment for him to realize who I was, being too timid to actually announce my name in those days. "I called? ...Ohh—hey, pal! That's right; I did call. I guess you got my message that I wanted to get a hold of you... Well,

there's some big news I thought you might be interested to hear about. Listen—you got a minute?" He effortlessly generated that feeling of honest-to-goodness warmth you get when "shootin' the breeze" with a longtime chum. What a thrill to hear that magical voice address me so personably!

"A few weeks ago, I was sitting in on this class; a kind of workshop for voice... basically for singers and people who want to do voiceovers—to improve their 'technique'... I was—well, kind of a guest speaker, and they wanted to hear all about my work, you know... It was at the studio of this great jingle composer Randy Van Horne; I don't know if you're familiar with him or not—you know him?" I didn't. "...and one of the students there, this young D.J.—Brian... ah, Cummings—he sort of took me aside after class, and was telling me that he felt, that he and a few of the others there weren't really getting into as much depth as they would like to with their acting skills, and they'd be interested in taking some private lessons with me, because Randy's field is really singing, you know..."

I began to wonder: Where's the exciting news? "...and I've been thinking lately that I'd really like to 'give something back' to the world. Well, it dawned on me that I probably could afford the time now... So, maybe it's time for me to 'try my hand' at teaching a group of students..." "Uh huh..." I had to let him know I was still listening, though I couldn't imagine how any of this applied to me. "I already have the studio out in back... I've always enjoyed writing for actors anyway... this really could be an ideal outlet for that—and I'd love to hear different voices reading the stuff, instead of just getting my own 'take' on everything—which you can only go so far with, y'know... I'm verbose, so that's 'a plus,' at least as far as teaching goes," we both laughed, knowing how he could 'gab' for hours on-end; "....And I just like the idea of 'molding young talent'... So basically, Brian and a few of the others from the group—that I feel are really 'the cream of the crop'—got me thinking about doing something myself along those lines, but more specifically focusing on acting... So I think we've got a really good group of students starting to take form, and I wanted to offer you a chance to be part of it as well."

I envisioned a 'naked in public' nightmare at the prospect of an "acting workshop". He continued his enthusiastic pitch: "We'll meet every Wednesday or Thursday, say 7 or 7:30—whatever night works best; we'll just have to see... after people are done with their 'straight' jobs...   I might even have to break it up into two nights if I get more than I can handle... I don't really know how it's going to go yet... But you think you might want to come?" Who—*me*? I thought. "Don't let me rush you, but I'd like you to at least consider it... You got a lot of raw talent, and I think you'd best be able to refine that in this kind of a workshop group setting... maybe even get you to come out of your shell a little... So, can I put you down for next week?"

A Workshop?! ...Group Setting?! I hesitated and stammered, stalling for time. "There's nothing to be nervous about—nobody's going to force you to read in front of everyone if you don't feel up to it... it's just here at the house... you remember how to get here, don't you?" "Ummm..." was all I could muster. "And if you're uncomfortable, or don't think you're getting anything out of it, you're not obligated to stay, you know..." "I mmmight be able to make it..." I waffled; but Daws knew full well that I was attempting to weasel out of it. "Well, I don't want to force you... and you know I wouldn't make you do anything if I didn't think it would be good for you... but I really think you should drop by, and at least just 'sit in' for a while, okay? ...So, see ya Thursday then: He did say I could leave if I wanted to... and since I never wanted to offend this magnificent friend, I finally agreed to show up... just this once, anyway. "Okay, buddy, so I'll see you then." He concluded in the voice of Mr. Jinx: "I think it's gonna be, like ah, a real gas, y'know—[cheeyuk yuk]." Jinxie's voice then relaxed into his own reassuring chuckle as he hung up the phone; sealing my fate for the next four and a half years.

the INNER SANCTUM

Making your way up the concrete pathway (formerly just a driveway) running along the right side of the lovely yet unassuming Beverly Hills home of Daws and Myrtis Butler, past the small patio with its canopy of flowering vines, you could see the festive light glowing from the open doorway of the converted two-story garage—now the hallowed headquarters of our voice acting "Boot Camp." As you approach the doorway, the animated "cocktail party" cacophony grows louder. The small crowd is milling about in the fairly large room, which modestly displays a smattering of select artifacts from Daws' wonderful career (gold records, animation cells, toys and knickknacks bearing the familiar likenesses of his cartoon personalities).

To the left, past the little piece of hallway that houses the staircase up to son Charles' room, is the thick, heavy door of the small, rectangular recording studio. It is outfitted in classic Radio Station style, with dark wood paneling coming halfway up the walls, in sharp contrast to the top half of the room, which was covered in old-fashioned cream colored "acoustic" tiles—those large square cardboard-like panels freckled with holes of varying small diameter arranged in an evenly scattered pattern. To your right, there are two large monitor speakers mounted up on the wall overhead, several feet above the extensive LP collection, smartly arranged and displayed in a retail store style bin; and in the middle of the opposite wall hangs a small drawn curtain. At the back of the room, perpendicular to those walls, another bulky door is taking up a considerable portion of the space at the left corner, and centrally located at eye level is the wide control room window peering in on a well maintained compliment of genuine vintage vacuum tube studio gear, complete with its awe-inspiring full-sized Ampex professional tape deck, poised just inside the gaping doorway. The back wall of the shallow booth bears an expanse of sturdy shelves which house The Master's reel-to-reel tape library, the box spines all labeled in his familiar scrawl. In the center of the wood parquet tiled floor of the recording space looms the huge and heavy stands which suspend the impressively substantial classic RCA ribbon microphones from the thick chrome arms of their fishing pole booms. Wow. But not now... Recording will come later. Maybe months later, after our lessons have begun to 'take root.'

For now, it's back to the workshop area, as we gravitate towards our informally chosen folding chairs surrounding the long dark table set up in the center. There are the usual meeting room compliments of canned sodas, cookies, candies, nuts and other snacks laid out in bowls and trays scattered about, and the traditional West Bend coffee maker and Solo Cups set up on a snack table near the "garden variety" sofa, upon which sat the proud parents of our younger students or the occasional observer. Daws calls for us all to settle down, and is seated at the head of the table.

Before him is a stack of his own cleverly penned scripts, which are then passed around to all the participants. His writing is purposely difficult to get a 'handle' on; carefully crafted to be open to a nearly infinite range of interpretation. A genuine *exercise* which actors must first struggle to decode, then apply great depth of imagination and creativity in a complex exploration of character and emotion, through a virtual rainbow of possibilities.

"Okay… Once you've all had a chance to look it over… If anyone feels they'd like to start off… When you feel you're ready. Any ideas? …Anyone? If not I'll just pick someone." Perhaps someone sheepishly volunteers. (the first brave soul is usually female, I recall). "It's just a cold read, so no one expects you to be great. Just terrific, is all." he chuckles. "No pressure here…okay?" then, with great authority, he lays out the workshop's 'credo': "…But *don't be afraid to be lousy*: that's the only rule here." He looks over to the now eager volunteer, scans the table thoughtfully, and calmly selects the others who will round out the cast for the cold read. (If it was a monologue, he'd line up 4 or 5 students to read in succession) "Just dive right in. No pressure…" Others suddenly decide they'd like to give it a try. "Don't worry, everyone who wants to will get a chance to read. But let's just hear this group for now… then we'll go over it together, and after that we'll do it again with whoever else wants to give it a try. …Okay?" He tentatively nods to the first group with a half-smile.

Daws would first listen to the reading without interrupting, unless prompted by the students themselves. They read the scene straight through. All eyes refer back to our mentor. "Any comments?" Some of the classmates might make a remark or two about what they'd heard. Those who just performed make some apologetic or politely defensive remarks. "That's all valid…" was his general response, which would be followed by his own commentary on the performances—always expressed in the positive, with suggestions on how to make it better next time. "Okay, now I'd like to show you how I was thinking this might be interpreted…"

Then, with the polished sincerity of a master craftsman, Daws himself would brilliantly show us 'how it's done'; first straight through, as he imagined it when he wrote it, and then "tossing it around" with us—all the while frequently stopping to illustrate, often by giving an assortment of skillfully executed variations to each line's delivery, the reasons why he would give a particular line the specific "shading" he'd just demonstrated. He would ask questions we should be thinking about as he reread each phrase with his unique "line-by-line" commentary. Let me give you my own made-up example of how he went over the lines with us…

"I think I'd better close the door." Why is he closing the door? Is he embarrassed about what he's going to say to her, and afraid someone might hear? Does he suddenly realize that he always forgets to close it, when she had repeatedly warned him that the cat would get out? "I think I *better close the door*" giving it a falling inflection, showing her he knows she was just about to scold him for leaving it open again. …or he could be getting a subconscious signal from her that she would like to get 'intimate' with him: "I… *think* I… ah… better close thee, ah… *door*." Or maybe he sees a nosy neighbor out on the sidewalk, that he doesn't want interrupting his date: "I think I better close the *door*." …notice the rising inflection there? "close the d*oorr*" …see, it's almost like a question; like, "Uh oh, that idiot across the street is coming over to mess up my evening again, so I better close the door this time…" And you wanna "tumble" those words, like you really gotta go to the bathroom. Not quite panic, but if you don't get up and do it right now you're really gonna regret it! See?…" In this way, Daws showed us how to convey not just the apparent meaning of the words (what is intentionally being said, enabling the listener to clearly follow what is going on in the scene), but also the emotions and logic behind each thought the character expresses—the imagined sub text that betrays the true feelings and internal thought processes which invariably exist below the surface of the dialogue. Not a great example, but that is basically how he'd go over a script with us.

Once every line and possible detail was fully explored in this manner, the script would then be reassigned among the students, who would take what they had just learned and hopefully apply it to their performances. Then more review and comments. Perhaps another group or two would then perform the scene. After everyone—who wanted to—had their turn reading it, another script would be passed around the table, and the process would start over again. There might even be a third script, if things were really 'cookin' that night.

After a "potty break," we'd reassemble around the table to toss around ideas and lively conversation, maybe try something we hadn't thought of before, then gradually dissolve, as the group members began to head home. There were always a few "stragglers" who would continue gabbing into the 'wee hours,' slowly meandering out to the sidewalk next to our dew-shrouded parked cars, for continuing gusts of extended conversation and heartfelt hugs shared with our mentor. I was always among the last of these, never wanting it to end, no matter that it was already 2 AM on a weeknight. Hey, what could possibly have been more important, anyway?

WHAT I LEARNED

Voice Acting is all about "getting the words off the page": Performing the dialogue not by simply reading aloud, but delivering the lines as if those words just naturally occurred to the character; as an expression of that character's own thoughts and feelings at that particular moment in their imaginary lives.

Love the words, but don't fall in love with them (or the sound of your own voice). "Taste" the words: they are delicacies to enjoy, but try not to let the listener hear you 'savoring' them too often. Becoming too attached to the words **exactly as they appear on the page** will often create a stilted and mechanical performance, trapping the actor in a limited or unnatural range of expression.

It is far more important to express the emotion behind the word, than to actually feel that emotion while you're doing it; and clearly sounding the word is not really necessary for the listener to know it's there: so long as the meaning and emotion behind the word is clearly communicated within the context of the speech.

Voice Acting is very much like Jazz: The words represent the melody, but are open to "interpolation." They may be molded, changed or enhanced as your character would see fit. Nothing is "written in stone." So long as the intention, or meaning, is the same, you are not showing any disrespect for the writer by making the words "your own."

As with music, the timing and pauses between words and phrases can be just as important as the words themselves. A prime example would be Jack Benny, of whom it was said that his greatest or funniest moments in front of the microphone... were silence.

Mediocre or insecure writers, directors and producers may prohibit you from taking these 'liberties' with their script, but strive for it anyway. When they hear how much life you've brought to the character, they may lose some of that paranoia about "touching" or "losing" some of the writer's 'precious jewels' on the page, and actually appreciate your contribution to the synergy of the production.

Also just like making music, you are part of the ensemble. You are not the entire show, so it is vitally important to place yourself among all the other 'threads' which make up the 'fabric' of the production. Be professional, polite and prepared. Respect everyone else involved in a project, especially the writers. If you separate your performance from everything else in that hypothetical "cloth," the whole thing falls apart. When you allow everyone else to be their best, your best will shine through to its fullest potential.

Voice Acting comes from your entire body. If only your mouth is moving, that's all anyone will hear. While taking care to stay 'on mic' and not generate any other noise in the studio, freely use facial expression, hands and body in a naturally instinctive manner while you are reading your lines, no matter how silly you may think you look to the others in the room. Since the audience will never see you anyway, inhibiting your physical expression is not only unnecessary, but will invariably inhibit your vocal performance as well.

Forget about your own voice: let the *character* deliver the lines. If you are thinking about yourself, and how *you* sound, you will prohibit the character from expressing itself, making the listener aware that you are simply manipulating your voice in a hollow attempt to sound like someone else.

There is no one definitive way to deliver anything. If it's good and it works, then it is perfectly valid. (Once again, mediocre directors may only allow the specific reading they have "formulated" in their heads to be considered "right"; making any other choice "wrong" in their opinion. This is, unfortunately, all too common these days.)

Avoid giving a "cosmetic" reading: The standard, tried'n'true, expected, pedestrian interpretation which 90 percent of the world's actors normally deliver. Be thoughtful and inventive with how you use and deliver your character's dialogue, with respect to "What am I actually trying to communicate?" and "How do I really feel in this situation?". If you are cliché in your readings, your work will be bland and undistinguished—and ultimately forgotten along with the rest of the uninspired background noise of the world.

LIFE'S LESSONS

"They're gonna do what they're gonna do." Outraged when I heard that the ad agency was auditioning people to replace Daws Butler as the voice of Cap'n Crunch, I called him up, urging him to take some kind of action to stop this unjustified absurdity—and *that* was his disarmingly calm and simple response. In that instant, I suddenly 'got it': that you can only do your best, and accept whatever comes of it; don't waste your time and energy attempting to fight decisions that are truly out of your hands. By the way, Daws never was replaced as Cap'n Crunch in his lifetime.

That statement, I feel, best exemplifies the timeless wisdom he dispensed; which has helped me immeasurably in life. I also fully realized other Universal Truths from his exemplary presence as a Great Human Being:

Daws treated ALL people with the same respect and openness; with humility and goodwill: He literally could not have cared less about anyone's religion, sexuality, ethnicity, politics, or their use of drugs or booze. Rich or poor—no matter what kind of car you drove or home you lived in—all were welcomed graciously: Even those who couldn't come up with the very reasonable dues for the workshop were never turned away, allowing those who were "strapped for cash" to continue their studies at a generous discount for as long as the situation lasted (sometimes 'letting it slide' completely, without making a 'big issue' over it). He saw outward appearance as merely a container for a person's character; not a particularly positive or negative reflection of it—and aside from being "well groomed," made no attempts to impress people with his choice of apparel. "Nobody really cares how you're dressed anyway," he'd remark. "They're only worried about how they look to the world. ...So I just dress for comfort."

Along those same lines, he proved that you could do monumental things—even at a mere 5 feet 2 inches tall; reaffirming the idea that size doesn't really matter all that much. And even though no "Matinee Idol," he 'lit up the room' with his gorgeous spirit. He had an ironic sense of humor about his own appearance, once telling me that I could verify that I knew him (to someone expecting a call from me) by describing him as "tall and extremely handsome". He wasn't the least bit offended by my gales of laughter which followed—he laughed just as heartily.

He never actively sought fame and fortune, and wasn't impressed by those things at all. He saw them as show business games, and a poisonous distraction from a healthy and satisfying life spent creating lasting works of art and entertainment; that 'being The Star' has nothing to do with the pursuit of genuine artistic achievement—and helping others to "shine" will benefit you most of all (again, I'm reminded of Jack Benny). He didn't even see any point in commenting about the lack of recognition shown him for the significant creative contributions he provided to the early success of so many he'd worked closely with over the years (such as Stan Freberg and Hanna/Barbera). Never resorting to lawsuits or raising a huge fuss to command attention, Daws Butler felt that if you just kept doing good work, you will eventually reap the sweetest rewards from your efforts. As he put it: "The rest is all bullshit.".

Good Writing is at the heart of good Acting. Expert selection of words, together with how they are applied in the context of the storytelling, is vitally important to the creation of great characters. Words often mean a lot more than they seem to on the surface. And while everyone agrees that show business is not for the faint of heart, acting which exposes emotional sensitivity is not for "sissies" either (along with other forms of human expression).

Art is Art: whether it be any type of performing, painting, sculpting, writing, cooking, designing products or architecture—it all comes from the soul of an Artist. While he didn't care for the "noise" of music that wasn't Classical or Jazz, he appreciated the poetry and emotion expressed in all forms of music. It was all "valid" to Daws, and he respected the integrity of all sincere artistic endeavors, even if it was offensive to his own sensibilities or personal taste. I remember my mentor every time I feel the urge to put-down rap or hip hop music: that no matter how distasteful I may find it, it's still an honest creation of artistic expression that should be assessed fairly, and with respect. All forms of Art should be "given its' due." ...Anything other than the thoughtless or cynical manipulation of an unwary public to earn a "quick buck," that is.

Do it Anyway: You really can do what you aim to. It doesn't matter if there's money in it for you, or awards, or fame. And no matter what negative declarations people make, or what anyone might say about you, there's always a way to "make it work." ...Because, after all, *They're gonna do what they're gonna do.* ...So why not just "Do it Anyway"?

LOVE THE PEOPLE AND THINGS THAT ARE TRULY WORTHWHILE
LIFE IS TOO SHORT TO BE WASTED
ENJOY IT ALL.

— *Corey Burton / Inspired by Charles Dawson Butler*

Preface

Daws wrote the scripts for his voice actors' workshop much like a composer, and orchestrator. His directions within the short scenes are not only fine-tuned (he would rewrite them over the years when additional exercises came to mind), but they are as precise as notes in a score. Every scene was constructed in order to enunciate just the right emotions out of the actors involved. To Daws, a period was quite different from a comma, a capitalized word in the middle of a sentence was to be vocalized in an alternate way to a lower-case word. O isn't read like Oh and this…doesn't make a (Pause).

Like any good playwright, Daws had a sense of character above all other things. Stresses, changes, all of these went to make an individual, a highly 3-dimension character, with room for the personality of the actor—always. Daws did not write for stereotypes.

Daws loved words as much as he loved sounds. That he had an impressive classical music collection is apparent in reading the way he wrote for his workshop students. His scripts are dotted with a variety of hints, as necessary as the dialogue itself.

UP – an increase in energy, not necessarily louder

DOWN – a decrease in energy, not necessarily softer

LOUD – an increase in volume

SOTTO – soft, under the breath

CHANGE – a shift in tone based on the thinking of the character

BEAT – the amount of time it takes to say the word "beat" in your head

"…" – let the previous thought trip over the next thought; a decay of the last word before the three dots, followed by a surge of energy on the word after the three dots.

PAUSE – stopping to think; length is based upon how the moment feels

THROW-AWAY – do not emphasize, underplay

LAYS IT OUT – emphasize, make a point

These instructions are only hints given by Daws. He expected the actor to start with them and look for new ways to say the words, new truths in the thought they implied. Daws felt the way to make a performance interesting was through orchestration, treating the script like a piece of music. Saying a phrase fast and then the next phrase slow, stretching out a line, mumbling a phrase, over articulating another, shouting one line and whispering the next, etc. These contrasts work but it does not matter so much where you do them as long as they feel right to you at the time. Daws would expect you to mark this book up, underline words you want to emphasize, draw a squiggly line over a word you want to stretch out, put parenthesis around a word or phrase you want to underplay, etc. Invent your own method of orchestrating your script. Once you have done this, use it only as a guide and follow your instincts to explore the many ways to say a line as you perform it.

The scripts speak for themselves. They are meant to be played with, to be, as the Master himself would say, bandied about. Practice these scripts, learn from them, rehearse them, use them as demos and auditions. But above all, understand the WORDS.

— The Editors

"I want you to understand the words. I want you to taste the words. I want to love the words. Because the words are important. But they're only words. You leave them on the paper and you take the thoughts and put them into your mind and then you as an actor recreate them, as if the thoughts had suddenly occurred to you."

— Daws Butler

The Writer and Actor and Mutual Orchestration

by Daws Butler

In all dialogue, the writer should indicate and the actor should be aware of: change-of-pace—rhythmic shadings—stress values—'throw-aways'—'tumbling' possibilities (short sentences read in tandem) and dynamic changes and inflection variants…which nourish the flow of natural continuity.

When I am 'directed' to just read the lines 'naturally' or '…just read it like yourself!' (whatever *that* means) I protest! After all, I didn't write the lines. They aren't mine. I really have nothing at all to do with them—except to give them 'life'—a God-like creation which must be kept in humble perspective. They belong to the character the writer has created—they are not the product of my thought-processes—they are figments of the writer's imagination and purpose—and I am to inherit his sensitivity. His lines, meaningful to him, must be intellectualized and visceralized (if you will) by me—and from my understanding of them, must come a fully formed comprehension—containing blood and bone and marrow—and hopefully a true scope of interpretation.

The writer's punctuation is not necessarily helpful—because there is no punctuation in spoken ideas. We don't imagine commas and periods and dynamics and pauses and thoughts, tumbling on top of each other—we are voice-prints of our own ability to articulate ideas.

The 'thoughts' behind a dramatic interpretation—which are to be read in a 'naturalistic' manner—are like aircraft—hovering in a 'holding pattern'—waiting for permission to 'come in'…Each one maintains its prescribed pattern and patiently waits, until—in proper progression—it contributes its part of the message to be conveyed—a happy landing!!

We do not read lines—we 'express thoughts'…in many instances, one 'thought' will wipe out another—it will take precedence, asserting its more valid importance to the continuity—this I would call 'decaying.' The end of one line seems to 'fall off' or atrophy—and the energy of the following line snaps into position. Its vitality is a refreshment—a transfusion—and it excites the listener, because it seems to be so 'natural' and spontaneous. Because it is representative of what happens in 'real life.' Remember—the actor's stock-in-trade is being 'real.' All else is pretension.

Let me give you an example of the 'decay.'

> She was in her room…the door was cracked…so I went in. She didn't look up. She mumbled something. (*Beat*)…so I just blurted it out…I told her how you felt…how you *really* felt. (*Beat*} She glanced up (*Decay coming!*) but kept right on packing…(*New energy*) *Talk* to her, Bill! Get up there and talk to her!

So what happened? 'Packing' became a dropped elision…and '*talk*' bit right on top of it!

Observation and sensitivity—that innate ability to take on the physical and vocal characteristics of someone else and to so lose one's self—is to become an actor. Talent is—in the classical sense, inborn (if one is so blessed). It begins as a small presence, waiting to be noticed. It needs only your expertise to nurture and maintain its function—to travel with its companions; observation, sensitivity, balance and adjustment.

Acting is impersonation—not of celebrities—but of the world we move in. It's people. Our own sensitivity and observation of life, accumulates over the years into a memory-bank—which can be drawn upon to supply the immediate prerequisites for the particular part we are to play—to give it naturalness, distinction and belief.

One's talent must be constantly fed—indifference can lead to its nutritional breakdown—until only a tiny fragment may remain—but even this fragment, like the 'starter' in a batch of sour-dough, can be revitalized—and regain its original potential.

It is your responsibility. You never stop growing… and knowing.

Exercises

Exercises

These were developed by Daws over many years of trial and error to prepare the lips, voice and emotions. Doing them on a regular basis will reap great benefits for the actor.

Warm Up Exercises

RESONANCE

Place the lips together lightly—make a tone—and blow through them. Try the tone on one note first. Be sure there is a tingling sensation in the lips and perhaps a tickling sensation also. The lips must be relaxed. When the tingling, ticklish sensation has been achieved, hum a tune. It is preferable to choose one with a fairly wide range of notes.

This exercise will give resonance to the voice and also clear the head and throat.

JAW RELAXATION

Let your jaw drop. Move it back and forth and up and down with your hand. Try to keep your jaw relaxed so that your hand can actually direct it.

Say the word "blah" fifteen times—keeping the jaw and throat muscles relaxed.

MOUTH FLEXIBILITY

Say "mmmmmm-EEEEEEEE-AH-OH-OO (MEOW)—Hum on the "m"—draw the lips back sharply for the "EEEEE" sound—open the mouth and throat wide for the sustained "AHHHHHHHHHHH"—Blend the "AHHHHHH" and "OHHHHHHHHH" and "OOOOOOOOO" together for a final pursing of the lips.

LIP FLEXIBILITY

Go through the alphabet, giving the consonant sound to the vowels, prefacing each one with "buh."

BUH BAY, BUH BEE, BUH BYE, BUH BOW, BUH BOO
BUH SAY, BUH SEE, BUH SIGH, BUH SEW, BUH SUE
BUH DAY, BUH DEE, BUH DYE, BUH DOUGH, BUH DO
(CONTINUE WITH F-G-H-J-K-L-M-N-P-Q-R-S-T-V-W-Y-Z)

TONGUE FLEXIBILITY

Say a series of "LA's" as rapidly as possible. LALALALALALALALA. Sing a song, using "LA" instead of words.

General—Plosives and Sibilants

It may seem pretentious to pretend to be a paragon when it comes to plosives and sibilants—one declines (in modesty and honesty perhaps) to accept the label of connoisseur. Interesting word 'connoisseur'—I wonder if you, seemingly as a sub-subject for a salutary address, intended for a salutary purpose, might single out a single citizen as being a person of 'connoisseurity'—Is 'connoisseurity' a rub-off of 'connoisseur?' This is not the essential concern of this systematic, yet realistic writer. One writes what one feels—if creativity is the prerogative—and not the mundane—Celebrate, in song and story, the sustenance the muse will bring—the mental manna, that affixes itself like mucilage to the mind—to be translated later to the starving psyches of the forthright but unfeeling, non-cerebral, finite, minds of the multitudes. Who can predict, with any certainty, the success of this supposition, in proving the particular points presented?

Exercises For Plosives and Sibilants
(Man)

Hello, Paula?—Petey. It's about Paul. Paul practically forced me to tell you my symptoms—simply because he worries about me so much. Like you said the other day, it's a pity he can't practice anymore. But when you peak in your career as he did, well…you slow down. It's so senseless of him to second-guess a possible new success. Paul's eighty-six and God knows he still probably has several years of dedicated and determined work left in him—but Myra's set her sights on that safari in Samaraland this summer and Paul's not going to weasel out of it this semester! Not if I know Myra! Anyway, Paul said I should pick my own doctor—he doesn't particularly care if it's Prentiss or Bolcher. Knowing Paul and his penchant for precedent, he'd prefer Prentiss. He considers Bolcher an upstart—even now when Bolcher is seventy! Prentiss, Prastissy and Bolcher. The big three. (Paul always hated our family name – Prastissy.) (*Change*) At any rate, Paula, I told Paul, plainly and to the point, that I wanted a woman doctor. No buts. I dig this women's lib thing and besides women are more compassionate. This was a bitter pill for Paul to swallow. He's always questioned the wisdom of the creator in allowing women to bear children! Badly organized lot, he said. Men were the logical choice. But Paula, before Paul pretends, on some pretext or other, that he never talked to me about medical help, please see that Suzie sizes up the situation and puts me down in the appointment book. There's nothing wrong with me, but if Paul wants to put up the pazoozas for my exam—it seems sensible to me to have you benefit by his petty bullheadedness. Think about it and buzz me back, pronto! O.K.? Bye.

Temperaments
(Woman or Man)

(Softly)   I'm speaking quite softly now...because I'm not sure who's listening. It might be someone who'd resent my being here...although I'm within my rights to be here...

(Confident)   Of course I'm within my rights! I'm here, because I was asked. I fear no one. I have nothing to hide. I am a strong, dominant personality. If there's any question in your mind, step forward and declare yourself! I challenge you!

(Fright)   Wait! Don't step forward! Please wait! I didn't realize what I was saying...forget what I said...if you suspect...I mean, even slightly...that I'm here under false pretenses, I'll leave! I'm terrified of conflict!

(Puzzled)   ...now why'd I say that? A moment ago, I expressed great confidence and then insecurity and fear. Why? There must be a logical reason...but why?

(Sorrow)   I know why...it's me. I'm to blame. No one else. I've tried to be someone other than myself. I deeply regret this. I'm ashamed!

(Happy)   No, I'm not! Why should I, of all people, be ashamed? I'm a nice person! Really, I am! Talented, attractive, wealthy. Charitable. (*Up*) I give crumbs to hungry birds...fish to hungry cats...and money to hungry millionaires! I'm happy at last...and you know why? Because this is the end of the monologue!!

Dialogues

Daws wrote many scripts featuring lovable Uncle Dunkle telling a story to his nephew Donnie. This one is a silly flight of fancy, yet it should be played as if Uncle Dunkle really believes what he is saying. Donnie, ever the questioning youth, enjoys the story so much he goes along with the gag.

BECAUSE AUNT RAPUNZEL WAS THERE
(2 Men, OR 1 Man, 1 Woman)

DUNKLE:	Donnie, have you ever wondered about your Aunt Rapunzel and me?
DONNIE:	Wondered about what?
DUNKLE:	About how we got together…how we became an 'item.'
DONNIE:	An 'item?' What's an 'item?'
DUNKLE:	It means that people noticed that we were seeing a lot of each other…that we only went out with each other.
DONNIE:	That's an 'item?'
DUNKLE:	Yeh.
DONNIE:	What about it?
DUNKLE:	Well, I mean, have you ever wondered what the magic was that made Aunt Rapunzel and I discover we were both residents of the same planet—and that our coming together was dramatically realized by a series of possibly unrelated circumstances
DONNIE:	Huh?
DUNKLE:	Did you ever wonder how Aunt Rapunzel and I got married?
DONNIE:	Yeh…but every time you tell me it's different somehow. I thought you just met each other somewhere…like at school, maybe…and you liked each other…and like that.
DUNKLE:	No, there was more to it than that. The very first time we set eyes on each other was at the top of Mount Everest. She was climbing up one side—and I was climbing up the other…and when I got to the top I looked across to the other side and I saw a pair of the most beautiful blue eyes I'd ever seen.
DONNIE:	Aunt Rapunzel?
DUNKLE:	No…her mule.

DONNIE:	(UP) Her mule!!
DUNKLE:	Yeh, the mule she was ridin' up to the top of Mount Everest.
DONNIE:	You don't ride a mule to the top of Mount Everest!
DUNKLE:	I know *I* didn't…but Aunt Rapunzel *did*.
DONNIE:	That's not what I meant.
DUNKLE:	It's what you said.
DONNIE:	No, I said…or maybe I should have said…you '*can't*' ride a mule to the top of Mount Everest.
DUNKLE:	There's a law against it?
DONNIE:	No, it's just impossible. There's too much snow and ice on the side of the mountain. The mule would slip and slide.
DUNKLE:	Donnie, your knowledge of mules is sadly misunderstood. Mules are sure-footed and have no fear of heights.
DONNIE:	Straight up?
DUNKLE:	What do you mean…'straight up?'
DONNIE:	I mean that there aren't little roads going up the mountain; you have to climb straight up sometimes. You have to have hands to place those little hooks in the cracks…and pull yourself up. A mule couldn't do that.
DUNKLE:	I don't want to go on and on about this. On second thought it was Aunt Rapunzel's beautiful blue eyes I saw.
DONNIE:	…and there wasn't any mule?
DUNKLE:	There wasn't any mule.
DONNIE:	Then why did you say there was?
DUNKLE:	I wanted to see if you'd believe it.
DONNIE:	I didn't.
DUNKLE:	So we dispense with the mule. Are you satisfied?
DONNIE:	Just tell me what really happened. I'm a little confused.
DUNKLE:	O.K. (*Pause*) As I said, I saw these beautiful blue eyes of Aunt Rapunzel—only I didn't know it *was* Aunt Rapunzel then—I just knew it was a beautiful blue mule…
DONNIE:	…lady.
DUNKLE:	A beautiful blue lady mule.
DONNIE:	No, just a beautiful blue-eyed lady. You said there wasn't any mule. Remember?
DUNKLE:	I remember. You got me sort of mixed up there. We both reached the top of Mount Everest at the same precise moment. So there wasn't any

question as to who got to the top first. We both did. And besides, the photos that the newspapermen took proved that we did.

DONNIE: What newspapermen?

DUNKLE: The ones on top of Mount Everest. You didn't think we would have climbed that dumb mountain if we weren't gonna get some publicity! You certainly didn't think that!

DONNIE: No, I guess I didn't think that.

DUNKLE: Anyway, Aunt Rapunzel and I got to talking and I asked if I could see her again and she said that would be O.K. So after we slid down Mount Everest to get to the bottom, we exchanged addresses and phone numbers.

DONNIE: Did you see each other again?

DUNKLE: You bet. She called me up the next morning—about three or four times.

DONNIE: Why so many times?

DUNKLE: I didn't answer the phone—so she kept calling.

DONNIE: Why didn't you answer the phone?

DUNKLE: Well, I was eating these caramels that was one of the prizes I got for climbing Mount Everest and I got some stuck in my tooth.

DONNIE: So you couldn't talk on the phone?

DUNKLE: So I couldn't talk on the phone, right. But she was really crazy about me and kept calling. Finally I managed to swallow all of the caramel and I answered the phone and it was him...

DONNIE: Him? Don't you mean 'her?'

DUNKLE: No, 'him'...it was the trainer of the mule. He was mad because he didn't get in any of the shots the newspapermen took.

DONNIE: I thought there wasn't any mule. You said there wasn't any mule.

DUNKLE: That's what I tried to tell the trainer. Then the other phone rang and I put the trainer on hold and who do you think was calling on the other phone?

DONNIE: Aunt Rapunzel.

DUNKLE: Aunt Rapunzel!! Our romance started right there. I made a date to go swimming with her in the pool in front of the Taj Mahal. We got a nice sun-tan and I asked her what she was doing the next day and she said she wasn't doing anything...so I said how about getting married.

DONNIE: And what'd she say?

DUNKLE: She said 'I thought you'd never ask!'

DONNIE: Why'd she say that?

DUNKLE:	Because I was eating the last caramel I had left from my Mount Everest climb and it was stuck in my tooth. When I finally swallowed it, I asked her. Took me a week and a half to swallow that darn caramel!! I was sick of caramels!! And I told that to Aunt Rapunzel…and she said she had something better for me—something I'd like. And I did!
DONNIE:	Mustard fudge.
DUNKLE:	Right! Mustard fudge! So the next day we got married and that's the true story of how Aunt Rapunzel and I got together. Any questions?
DONNIE:	Just one. What happened to the mule trainer?
DUNKLE:	Don't ask me. He's probably still on hold!

[This is Daws' tribute to Abbott & Costello routines such as "Who's on First?" There is great opportunity to use what Daws called "fast against slow," "loud against soft" changes of pace and dynamics. It should have the snappy vaudeville quality but should not rushed.]

BLUR-BLUR
(2 Men or Woman)

BLUR: Excuse me. {*Beat*) Excuse Me!

OTHER: Why?

BLUR: Huh?

OTHER: You do something wrong?

BLUR: No.

OTHER: Well, I didn't say you did.

BLUR: What I said was 'Excuse me.'

OTHER: …and I said 'Why? You do something wrong?'

BLUR: Actually, I didn't mean that kind of 'excuse me'…(*Sotto*) Something is being complicated here which is really very simple. (*Up*) What I wanted to do, was get your attention so I could ask you a question.

OTHER: Why'd you have to attract my attention? Didn't you see…weren't you aware of the look of revulsion on my face?…I saw you!

BLUR: Well, you know, I just figured…

OTHER: You're the one who wanted to ask the question, not me! (*Up*) So why're you getting hostile?

BLUR: Huh?

OTHER: You're the one who started the whole thing!

BLUR: Actually, all *I* said was…

OTHER: (*Up*) O.K! O.K! Somebody's gotta back down, it might as well be me. (*Beat*) You wanted to ask a question? (*Lays it out*) What…is…the question?

BLUR: D'you find it difficult relating to people? (*Clears throat*) What I really wanted to ask is…will you tell me a story?

OTHER: A story?

BLUR:	A story.
OTHER:	I don't tell stories very well. No flair. Some people have a flair. I don't have a flair.
BLUR:	Tell me a story anyway. I just won't enjoy it.
OTHER:	That sounds fair, even without a flair. (*Change*) Now, I haven't the slightest interest, but first of all, what's your name?
BLUR:	Blur Blur.
OTHER:	What?
BLUR:	Blur Blur.
OTHER:	Sounded like you said 'Blur Blur.'
BLUR:	Blur Blur.
OTHER:	Blur Blur?
BLUR:	Blur Blur.
OTHER:	Blur Blur what? What's your last name?
BLUR:	Blur Blur.
OTHER:	Blur Blur is your *last* name?
BLUR:	It's the last name I had.
OTHER:	I'll accept that. (*Clears throat*) Once upon a tine there was a boy named Jack.
BLUR:	Jack who?
OTHER:	Just Jack…lotsa stories start out with a boy named Jack.
BLUR:	George is better. Why couldn't his name be George?
OTHER:	Because when they dumped the water on his head, they baptized him Jack…not George. (*Beat*) Will you accept Jack?
BLUR:	Well, you know, I…
OTHER:	You'd rather it was George?
BLUR:	I'd rather.
OTHER:	I'll make a deal with you. I'll say Jack. You 'think' George. O.K?
BLUR:	O.K.
OTHER:	Once upon a time there was a boy named Jack.
BLUR:	George.
OTHER:	I said think it!
BLUR:	I was thinkin' out loud.
OTHER:	I'll accept that. (*Up*) Jack and his mother were very poor. One day…when they were sitting around starving, she told him to go sell the cow.

BLUR:	Why?
OTHER:	So they'd have money to buy milk.
BLUR:	Why didn't they get it from the cow?
OTHER:	That…is a stupid question!
BLUR:	Why?
OTHER:	The cow didn't have any money!
BLUR:	I'll accept that.
OTHER:	So what Jack did, he went to town…bought the cow a couple burritos…and one for himself.
BLUR:	Umm, yummy…burritos (*Up*) Where'd he get the money?
OTHER:	From the cow…
BLUR:	But you said…
OTHER:	The cow lied. (*Change*) So Jack sold it to a guy for two hundred dollars, took the money home, gave it to his mother…less the seventy-five cents he hadda pay the cow for the burritos…and she invested what was left in real estate and they became independently wealthy. (*Up*) The end. Ta-daaaah!
BLUR:	That's the story?
OTHER:	That's the story! (*Beat*) You enjoy it?
BLUR:	No.
OTHER:	No?
BLUR:	I told you I wouldn't enjoy it—but I didn't think I'd enjoy it that *little*.
OTHER:	What was wrong with the story?
BLUR:	It…it lacks conflict. It has no social significance. (*Up*) Let's us develop a *real* story! For openers, let's say George.
OTHER:	Jack…
BLUR:	George.
OTHER:	Jack!!
BLUR:	*George*! Jack was the guy in your story. George is the guy in my story.
OTHER:	I'll accept that.
BLUR:	So let's accept the premise that George sold the cow for…some magic beans.
OTHER:	Magic beans?
BLUR:	George plants 'em and they grow into this huge beanstalk. George climbs to the top of it…and discovers a giant's castle. He knocks at the door.

OTHER: Wudja stop for?

BLUR: I just roughed out the basic story-line. You take it from here.

OTHER: The door opens…and it's the giant's wife—she lets him in. Tells him the giant is real mean and doesn't bathe very often.

BLUR: This is gettin' good!

OTHER: Your turn!

BLUR: They hear the giant coming…he's sayin' 'Fee Fi Fo Fum—I smell the blood of an English*mum*!'

OTHER: Mum? Did you say 'Mum?'—Don't you mean 'English*man*?'

BLUR: No, 'Mum!'…The giant doesn't dig a sloppy lyric.

OTHER: I'll accept that! (*Beat*) So how does the story end?

BLUR: George learns about the magic harp that composes music…and the goose that lays golden eggs…and he sweet-talks the giant into buyin' out a major label with the golden eggs…

OTHER: Yeh, and then the magic harp records some hits that go right to the top of the charts…

BLUR: …and he and the giant clean up!! The end! Ta-daaah!
            (*Both laugh*)

OTHER: …and Jack's mother—what'd she get?

BLUR: An autographed picture of Doc Severinson…in a business suit.

OTHER: Aw, you blew it! Up to now the story was believable!!

[This is an exercise in alliteration and timing. It should have a bouncy, playful feel to it, fast-paced but without over-playing the lines. Try to complete the scene in exactly thirty seconds while still getting the most out of every line.]

THE LI'L BITTY BIT
(2 Men)

BART:	Hey, Bert!
BERT:	Yeh, Bart?
BART:	We both gotta bang out a thirty-second bit, Bert…and no 'buts.'
BERT:	No 'buts' about the bit?
BART:	No 'buts.'
BERT:	…and what's the 'no buts bit' about, Bart?
BART:	The bit's about a boat, Bert. A big broad-bottomed butter-barge.
BERT:	O.K. Bart, we'll both bust our britches to bring off a lil bitty thirty-second bit about a big, broad-bottomed butter-barge, *while we button up our boots, Bart!*
BART:	Our brown, bulky, bargain, store-boughten boots, Bert?
BERT:	You bet, Bart. Boots!
BART:	Oh! Oh!—it's a bother, Bert, but better than blow the bit, I better blurt out what's being bandied about…the brown, bulky, bargain, store-boughten boots are *already* buttoned up!!
BERT:	They better be! 'cause that's the thirty-second bit!!

[Imagine your frustration in trying to tell this simple well-known tale and being interrupted with logic at every turn.]

THREE BEARS
(2 Men or Women)

ONE:	Once upon a time there were three bears.
TWO:	How d'ya know?
ONE:	There just were. Papa, Mama and the baby bear. They lived in a house in the woods…
TWO:	Whose house?
ONE:	Their house, of course.
TWO:	Bears don't live in houses. They live in caves.
ONE:	Well, then, it was a cave.
TWO:	Cave, I'll accept.
ONE:	One morning. Mama bear made some porridge…
TWO:	Hold on! Not so fast there! Bears can't cook…
ONE:	Well, this one could…
TWO:	And bears don't eat porridge—berries. They eat berries.
ONE:	O.K.—the mama bear fixed up a big bowl of berries—then she said. "These berries are too hot—let's go for a walk in the woods till they cool off."
TWO:	How'd the berries get hot?
ONE:	They were on the stove.
TWO:	What stove?
ONE:	The bear's stove.
TWO:	Bears don't have…
ONE:	So they went for a walk and a little girl came up to their house…
TWO:	Cave.
ONE:	Cave—and her name was Goldilocks.

TWO:	That's not a name.
ONE:	Well, it was her name and…
TWO:	What was her real name? Mary? Louise? Hephzibah? What?
ONE:	Her name was…I'll just call her the little girl. O.K.?
TWO:	…uh…O.K.
ONE:	She ate some of papa bear's berries and said, "Oh! these berries are too hot!"
TWO:	How'd they get hot?
ONE:	Never mind! Then she tried mama's berries and they were too cold!
TWO:	Were they in the refrigerator?
ONE:	Right! The refrigerator.
TWO:	Bears don't have refrigerators.
ONE:	Then she tried the baby bear's berries and they were—just right—and she ate 'em all up!
TWO:	That's stealing. They weren't her berries—they could put her in the pokey for that.
ONE:	Well, they didn't. Then she broke the baby bear's chair.
TWO:	Bears don't sit on chairs.
ONE:	O.K.—she didn't break the baby bear's chair. She went to sleep on his bed!
TWO:	A pile of old leaves, huh?
ONE:	(*Sigh on the word*) Yeh – then the bears came home from their walk and they found what Goldilocks had done…
TWO:	Who?
ONE:	The little girl and…
TWO:	And they ate her all up!
ONE:	Right—they ate her all up!
TWO:	That's a good story. G'nite!!

[This is Daws' tribute to or parody of Samuel Becket's Waiting for Godot. *Even though the characters are saying outlandish things, they believe very strongly in what they are saying and you must play them with utter and serious conviction.]*

GODOT (NOT HOME) REVISITED
(2 Men)

D'USSEAU:	Damen!
DAMEN:	Yes, D'Usseau?
D'USSEAU:	(*Spreads hands*) See?
DAMEN:	See what?
D'USSEAU:	Look around you!
DAMEN:	(*Sound of disgust*)
D'USSEAU:	I've brought you all my fish!
DAMEN:	(*Shrugs*) All your fish?
D'USSEAU:	(*Spreads hands*) All! All the fish I've pulled from the great sea.
DAMEN:	Tell me more about these fish. Nothing biographical. Don't bother with individual personality traits…just some of their general characteristics.
D'USSEAU:	(*Doubtful*) You're referring to the fish?
DAMEN:	I am.
D'USSEAU:	Some of the fish…now slopping over your boots…are green.
DAMEN:	Green?
D'USSEAU:	Green. Some are red.
DAMEN:	Green and red?
D'USSEAU:	Green and red. Some are white…and glisten…this is evidence of recent life.
DAMEN:	(*Up*) You mean they're deceased? Passed over? Certified fertilizer-fodder? You mean they're dead?
D'USSEAU:	(*Offended*) Did I say they were dead?
DAMEN:	No.

D'USSEAU:	Well then! (*Quickly*) Some of the fish I cleaned and some I didn't.
DAMEN:	How many did you clean?
D'USSEAU:	(*Softly*) Most of them I didn't clean.
DAMEN:	(*Up*) How *many* did you clean?
D'USSEAU:	(*Quickly*) All of them I didn't clean!
DAMEN:	All?
D'USSEAU:	All!
DAMEN:	All of them you didn't clean!
D'USSEAU:	Truth…is essential in matters of no importance. (*Up*) Take the fish you want, Damen! Take them all! I don't want any!
DAMEN:	Nor I!…I find your gift repugnant.
D'USSEAU:	(*Hurt*) I see. (*Pause*) I neglected to tell you something, Damen.
DAMEN:	My generous nature will absorb your over-sight, D'Usseau…I release you from any commitment.
D'USSEAU:	I cannot accept such a release…I must tell you! All of the fish are mackerel.
DAMEN:	All?
D'USSEAU:	(*Hands spread*) All!
DAMEN:	Let's go back a bit, D'Usseau…earlier, you referred to the fish as vari-colored…do you recall that?
D'USSEAU:	I do.
DAMEN:	Green and red is not vari-colored—it is merely green and red—one additional color does not qualify for the use of the term 'vari-colored.'
D'USSEAU:	Are you sure?
DAMEN:	You could look it up. (*Up*) You said before that 'truth is essential in matters of no importance'…is your statement not un-important enough for truth?
D'USSEAU:	It is, Damen! Indeed it is!
DAMEN:	Then I expect an immediate apology!
D'USSEAU:	Of course you do!…I apologize!! I (*Change—urgent*) Now take your green and red fish, Damen…and be off!
DAMEN:	No!
D'USSEAU:	No?
DAMEN:	Mackerel are too bony for me—I can't abide bones—to me, one bone is maximum! (*Goes on*) Another thing, D'Usseau—have we discussed the taste of the mackerel?

D'USSEAU:	Not as yet…no.
DAMEN:	Up to now, we have ignored completely…that aspect of the mackerel. (*Up*) Personally, I find the taste of the mackerel…not 'casual.'
D'USSEAU:	Not 'casual?'…Why is the taste not 'casual?'
DAMEN:	…because, (*Chuckle*) because it comes on 'too strong!'
D'USSEAU:	(*Lightly*) A pretty metaphor, indeed! A darling metaphor!
DAMEN:	Also…there is nothing about the mackerel that is…'exemplary!'
D'USSEAU:	Exemplary?
DAMEN:	…above reproach!
D'USSEAU:	(*Chuckle*) Another darling metaphor!
DAMEN:	Mackerel are reproachful all the way. (*Up*) The substantiation of my statement is available if you care to research it…
D'USSEAU:	It's documented?
DAMEN:	(*Up*) Did I say it was documented?
D'USSEAU:	(*Mollified*) No. (*Pause*) Is it?
DAMEN:	Yes…So what I said was not based on personal pique.
D'USSEAU:	Let's get back to the mackerel.
DAMEN:	*We've never left them.* Their stench assails the nostril. (*Shudders*)
D'USSEAU:	(*Annoyed*) Why did you shudder?
DAMEN:	(*Measured*) I wish they wouldn't 'stare' like that!!!
D'USSEAU:	*It's the only way they know!* Their limited intelligence is incapable of variation and I find any contemplative evaluation of their optic attention inconclusive.
DAMEN:	True. A single word of description…or concern…is an extravagance.
D'USSEAU:	Before you were quibbling about bones…as if the mackerel were un-eatable.
DAMEN:	Inedible.
D'USSEAU:	Un-eatable…inedible…we're both saying the same thing.
DAMEN:	You see! I was right! An extravagance, as I said!
D'USSEAU:	(*Pause*) So…what about them?
DAMEN:	The fish?
D'USSEAU:	Who gets all the fish?
DAMEN:	You mean the mackerel?
D'USSEAU:	Of course, you dunderhead! Mackerel are fish!!
DAMEN:	In a generic sense at least.

D'USSEAU:	Then who gets all the mackerel? (*Quickly*) Actually, my question was rhetorical—I had already given them all to *you*.
DAMEN:	I don't want them.
D'USSEAU:	You don't want them—and I don't want them.
DAMEN:	...and as the activist of their present plight, you can't just walk away from them.
D'USSEAU:	It would be shirking my responsibility.
DAMEN:	It wouldn't be shirking *my* responsibility—so I'll walk away.
D'USSEAU:	And what will I do?
DAMEN:	You'll stay here, of course.
D'USSEAU:	...with the fish.
DAMEN:	...with the mackerel.
D'USSEAU:	Mackerel are fish!!
DAMEN:	I know. Mackerel are fish and fish are mackerel. (*Pause*) I'm leaving now...may I send you anything?
D'USSEAU:	Yes.
DAMEN:	What?
D'USSEAU:	Cats!!!!

[This is Daws' parody of Wallace Shawn's film My Dinner with Andre. *As with* Andre, *this piece is about two men who seem to have nothing in common, but yet somehow can carry on a conversation. Putsy is fascinated by "A" and "A" loves that Putsy is a good audience.]*

MY BRUNCH WITH "A"
(2 Men)

PUTSY: My name is Putsy, and I was on my way. I didn't take a cab. I walked. I was to have brunch with an old friend. My heart was pounding and I could feel cold sweat forming at my temples…it sizzled and dried up in the morning sun, so its dramatic significance was minimal…my remembrance of our past association told me that it wouldn't be that big a deal…we hadn't seen each other for several hours and I was curious to find out what had transpired in the life of "A." (My friend's name was "A.")…My destination was a non-descript coffee-house in the sixties that held many memories for us…One memory in particular was shared by us both…it had lousy coffee—but there were other memories, just as unpleasant, and I couldn't wait to hear my friend's voice, charming me with anecdotes that were mundane and untrue. (*Pause*) So I walked—it being the most primitive means of self-movement…not because it had any significance, but because I didn't have cab fare. (*Pause*) When I arrived, there was my friend waiting at a table. "A" was sitting in one chair and there was another across from him. Obviously mine…but I did inquire as to whether it was or not, because one can never be sure of anything in this topsy-turvy world. "A" had apparently been talking briskly, even before I arrived…"A's" entire life was programmed, and my being a few minutes late annoyed him…So, through my own fault, I had been cheated of hearing his vocal overture.

PUTSY: I'm here, "A."

"A": Finally! You missed my vocal overture.

PUTSY: I walked. It takes longer when you walk.

"A": You deprived yourself of several of my most exciting anecdotes, Putsy.

PUTSY:	Please continue with what you were saying.
"A":	I was talking about Vassily Tuponik.
PUTSY:	I don't know him.
"A":	Of course not! It's better that you don't.
PUTSY:	Why?
"A":	…because I treasure his friendship and I have never allowed myself to consciously share him with another.
PUTSY:	What about unconsciously?
"A":	Watch yourself! Your tardiness may yet enrage me!
PUTSY:	I'll watch myself.
"A":	Vassily Tuponik to those who know him well…
PUTSY:	(*Attacks*) Then there are others?
"A":	Yes, Putsy…and I resent them! Vassily is one of the most charming, unassuming…stupid…men I've ever known. He shares an empathy with everyone he knows.
PUTSY:	Is he friendly, urbane, outgoing?
"A":	You don't have to contribute to any of the points I made! Go peddle your adjectives in some other parish!!
PUTSY:	Go on.
"A":	It doesn't matter who he's talking to. It could be the supermarket checker…it could be somebody checking the air in his tires…or somebody to cash one of his worthless checks…or the Pope…
PUTSY:	You're not jealous of the Pope?
"A":	(*Goes on*) Everything works out fine with a conclusion that allows no coda!
PUTSY:	Coda?
"A":	Coda is a musical expression.
PUTSY:	I see. Go on.
"A":	I'm not through. A coda comes at the end of a musical work. A coda is a return to something the listener has already heard…
PUTSY:	I see. Go on.
"A":	…a reiteration…a dramatic effect in music. But this is unacceptable to Vassily and the termination of his scintillating *verbiage*. He says it once. That's it!!
PUTSY:	You say he's empathetic?
"A":	Empathetic…yes, that's the word to describe Vassily. Empathetic…*very* empathetic (*Quick*) or sometimes, just 'pathetic.'

PUTSY:	Vassily puts me in mind of a chap I once played lawn tennis with one summer in Shreveport, Louisiana before the famous hurricane.
"A":	What famous hurricane, Putsy?
PUTSY:	The one everybody knows about, "A."
"A":	*I* don't know about it.
PUTSY:	Look it up, sometime. It was a famous hurricane.
"A":	Hurricanes aren't famous. They're destructive…or horrendous. Movie stars are famous…
PUTSY:	…or chocolate chip cookies. (*Up*) The chap I'm referring to was named Emanuel Cupp…we talked a lot. We didn't have any particular penchant for the subjects we chose to discuss…but the long, leisurely evenings we spent on the fire-escape of his tenement, went on right up to the moment it was condemned, I don't wanna go on and on or reiterate, but I think that the point I've been trying to make has been made.
"A":	Obviously. When did all of this happen?
PUTSY:	Before the famous hurricane in Shreveport, Louisiana.
"A":	That was one humdinger of a hurricane. I got color slides of it for my birthday that year.
PUTSY:	You said you weren't aware of it…before, you said that.
"A":	Please, Putsy…let's not go on and on and on about this…or reiterate. What we learned from this encounter…was that an angry, Mother Nature kicked up her heels and gave us pause for thought. We've been over this. We're getting into a sort of reiteration here. I never intentionally reiterated, Putsy. (*Up*) But there are occasions when I *do* reiterate. I have a penchant for reiterating. (*Up*) I also have a penchant for saying 'penchant.'
PUTSY:	Why do you think that is?
"A":	I don't know…I'll check it out.
PUTSY:	Good!
"A":	I will most certainly get back to you on this.
PUTSY:	…on the penchant thing?
"A":	Right! (*Pause—5 counts*)
PUTSY:	What are you thinking about?
"A":	Is it really that important? The penchant thing, I mean? I've decided, that <u>I</u> *won't* get back to you on this.
PUTSY:	The penchant thing?
"A":	The penchant thing, right, I will let it go. (*Up*) Which is correct? *Let* it go or *leave* it go?

PUTSY:	…uh…well…
"A":	(*Quickly*) At any rate, I won't do it!!
PUTSY:	Not to change the subject…but are we gonna order anything?
"A":	I'd like that! (*Calls*) Waiter! Bring us food! It doesn't have to be gourmet…
PUTSY:	(*Softly*) I *like* gourmet.
"A":	(*Snaps*) Who asked you? (*Up*) Just bring anything that isn't creepy-crawly.
PUTSY:	So long.
"A":	Where you going?
PUTSY:	I've decided not to wait for our questionable repast, exciting and evocative as it might have been.
"A":	Why??
PUTSY:	Because never once in our relationship have I found you to be dundant.
"A":	This stuns me…I am hurt! Your accusation pains me, indeed! My well-being is shattered! I have been affected deeply by your sudden thrust of what must have been a long concealed contempt for me—although previously unexpressed. I am pained indeed!
PUTSY:	See what I mean? You're *not* dundant!!!

[Try playing this one as if the characters get tipsy as the piece goes on. Think about how long they have known each other and whether or not Derek cares about what Gary is saying.]

DIFFUSION
(2 Men)

GARY: I don't wanna go on the trip, Derek. I feel this weight in my chest when I even think about leaving. It's too much!

DEREK: You'll be back before you know it – what is it, two weeks?

GARY: Roughly. Could be longer – could be shorter too. (*Goes on*)

DEREK: Then...

GARY: ... I don't wanna invest even one second in however long it'll be! I'm just not gonna allow the chance of my not being here when she calls!

DEREK: (*Quietly*) *If* she calls.

GARY: You think she won't call?

DEREK: I don't say that... but she's making decisions.

GARY: You figure she's already made her decision?

DEREK: I said... 'decisions.'

GARY: It isn't just *me* she's concerned with? Is that what you're saying?

DEREK: Is that what it sounds like I'm saying? (*Pause*) Gary?

GARY: O God! You know where the short hairs are, doncha?

DEREK: You're obsessed with *her* – she isn't with *you*. It's so goddam obvious to everyone but you. She's determined, I think. Going to Venice is the dream she's always had. Diman Maas takes two new students every year. He's the premier colorist of the world – Fawn knows she's limited... but she also knows that she has this empathy with color .. graphics... she'll never know or be able to do anything about. She's out of it as far as graphics are concerned ... even form. She doesn't know – and doesn't really care about form – structure – All she cares about – and has any talent for – is diffusion.

GARY: .. and that's not just with painting. She diffuses it all. She diffuses her life and all the values it's got. Everything sort of flows together into a 'wash' …

DEREK: Fawn 'wants into' abstract film. Color moods with music.

GARY: It's nothing new. It's been *done*. What's the point?

DEREK: Not Fawn's way. *That's* the point, Gary .. you seem to be *missing* it all the time. Fawn ignores precedent.

GARY: Not 'missing' it .. avoiding it would be more like it! It seems so inconsequential!! She's got so goddamn little to offer! Why the hell does she have to go to Venice and study with Herr Maas .. how the hell he ever considered taking her on, is beyond me! One of two students, I mean!

DEREK: I don't think his reasons are based on her talent .. remember the party last Spring .. Myron's place in Malibu?

GARY: What about it?

DEREK: What about it? He spent the night with Fawn. You passed out as usual .. and got home .. the way you always get home, I guess – 'someway!' Anyway, Maas left with Fawn .. and when Myron called the next morning to ask Maas about something…

GARY: Yeh?

DEREK: Fawn answered the phone.

GARY: She'd been there all night?

DEREK: Unless it was a very early morning interview!…..Myron called about six .. he was leaving for San Francisco and had to be sure of where Maas was going to be for the next few days.

GARY: So you think they made love that night?

DEREK: They did something .. maybe their bodies got diffused.

GARY: Shut up!

DEREK: Look, Gary .. don't get me involved in your feelings for Fawn. To me, Fawn has always been a pain in the ass! If you could spread strudel-dough as thin as she spreads herself – 'diffuses' herself – you'd have the strudel lovers beating a path to your door!! Fawn wants to do everything .. she wants to *be* everything .. let's face it, Gary .. Fawn doesn't give a damn about you!

GARY: We'll see.

DEREK: (*Lays it out*) I'm going to level with you .. Fawn is damn good with color .. somewhere, along the line, it's gonna work for her .. maybe in fabrics .. who knows? She's determined. She *is* going to Venice.

GARY: She hasn't said so – definitely.

DEREK: You think she'll call you? Tell you what she's come up with? It's very inter-personal with her too .. Maas *may* want her 'bod' .. He

	probably does .. and he means to have it.
GARY:	Mass! .. that bastard!
DEREK:	He wants her money too .. and her old man'll put that up .. the shrinks have got him feeling guilty about what he didn't do for Fawn when she was a young chick .. so now he'll put out as much as she figures she wants. (*Change*) .. and let's get one thing straight – Fawn knows the old man is trying to get the 'Father of the Year' award .. but he only wants it from her. He's screwed up his own life .. all he's got left is Fawn. He's accumulated the 'gelt' .. she knows it. She'll take it – no questions asked.
GARY:	(*Thoughtful*) You think I might as well go to Chicago for the conference .. and if Fawn calls .. Fawn calls! If she doesn't .. that's my answer. I should go to Chicago, right?
DEREK:	Live your life, Gary. Fawn is gonna live hers.
GARY:	I want Fawn.
DEREK:	All you and Fawn have got in common is…what the hell *do* you hell in common?
GARY:	All I know is, she's figured in every TV Movie-of-the-Week I've written the past three years .. I see her in every line I write. I wished so damn much that she was an actress .. so I could write for her – I wanted her to be that malleable substance that I could mold and shape .. and it wouldn't have taken much .. I would have written it 'to her' … I know her so damn well .., or thought I did.
DEREK:	But she isn't an actress.
GARY:	She's a colorist. A dedicated 'colorist' … which is what?
DEREK:	It's like building a career on just being able to steal second base.
GARY:	(*Quietly*) So what do you think?
DEREK:	About what?
GARY:	I should go to Chicago?
DEREK:	If whatever there is between you and Fawn… means a damn thing .. yeh, I'd say go to Chicago.
GARY:	What if she leaves for Venice while I'm gone?
DEREK:	Only one thing you can do – check what the postage is for pouring out your 'first class' heart. If she loves you – really loves you – the 'not-hearing' from you will destroy her – regardless of her decision on going or staying .. and she'll come back to you.
GARY:	..and if she doesn't love me?
DEREK:	Then you're off the hook. You'll suffer .. but there won't be any more diffusion. Through a glass..brightly, Gary!

[Small talk at a party can be among the most difficult scenes to play. One way to breathe life into this piece is to ask yourself questions about how much the characters know about each other and the other guests at the party. For example, does Arnold know from the beginning that the women they are talking about is the boss' wife?]

A 'LIKELY' STORY
(2 Men)

ARNOLD: (*Looks around*) This…is one of those parties!

BRUCIE: How can you tell? We just got here.

ARNOLD: (*Chuckle*) I keep 'book' on boring parties. This is one of 'em.

BRUCIE: I get the idea that you put down most of the parties as boring.

ARNOLD: You're astute.

BRUCIE: Astute?

ARNOLD: Astute.

BRUCIE: What does 'astute' mean?

ARNOLD: Oh hell, you know what it means.

BRUCIE: No I don't.

ARNOLD: It just sounds like it means what it does. You mean, I gotta break it down for ya?

BRUCIE: (*Accuses*) You don't know what it means!

ARNOLD: It means sagacity.

BRUCIE: What does 'sagacity' mean?

ARNOLD: Gimme a break! I take it back—you aren't astute.

BRUCIE: What am I then?

ARNOLD: (*Up*) A pain in the ass! Look, all these parties are the same. Nod your head through the introductions. Size up a 'likely lay'…get smashed and find the likely lady and head for an unoccupied bedroom…

BRUCIE: Keep going!

ARNOLD: Get home somehow afterwards. Feel lousy the next morning…

BRUCIE: …and?

ARNOLD:	(*Tags it*) and hope the 'likely lady' hasn't got any plans for the future.
BRUCIE:	…and if she has?
ARNOLD:	Oh the hell with the likely lady!
BRUCIE:	I wish you'd introduce me to one! I like parties like this. Admit it, Arnold…people are going to parties every night! Celebrities go to be seen…
ARNOLD:	Didja ever think of this, Brucie?…about celebrities? About their 'day' and what it's like? Ordinary things…dull…routine…(*Up*) Like, can you imagine Marlon Brando drinking his coffee in the morning and reading the paper? Does he put on a robe or sit around in his underwear?
BRUCIE:	You mean he sleeps in his underwear?
ARNOLD:	He would have changed from his pajamas to his underwear…He had to go out and get the paper, right?
BRUCIE:	Then he'd probably put on his robe.
ARNOLD:	Probably.
BRUCIE:	Wait a minute…He's got servants, hasn't he?
ARNOLD:	One would think so.
BRUCIE:	One of them'd probably get the paper—and put the coffee on. (*Up*) You think he takes a bath in the morning? Maybe he takes a shower.
ARNOLD:	How about Genevieve Bujold?
BRUCIE:	You mean does she take a shower with Brando?
ARNOLD:	No. I mean what's her morning like? Does she look in the mirror and say 'O God!!' like every other woman in the world?
BRUCIE:	I wonder if she checks out her calluses when she's 'sitting?' (*Giggle*)
ARNOLD:	No. She would have told me.
BRUCIE:	(*Pause*) Arnold…
ARNOLD:	Yeh?
BRUCIE:	…over there!
ARNOLD:	Huh?
BRUCIE:	(*Quickly*) Don't look! I'll tell you when. There's a woman over there and she's been giving me the 'eye!' (*Quickly*) *Now look*! (*Beat*) You see her?
ARNOLD:	Yeh.
BRUCIE:	You think she might be a 'likely?'
ARNOLD:	*Not* likely!

BRUCIE:	Why not?
ARNOLD:	...because I spotted her when we first came in.
BRUCIE:	You recognize her?
ARNOLD:	Yeh. I probably should have spoken to her.
BRUCIE:	Why'd you say that she's not a 'likely?'
ARNOLD:	I mean she's not 'likely' for *you*.
BRUCIE:	(*Up*) Well, the hell with *you*! I'm goin' over and talk to her. I came here tonight to score...so you just stay out of it!
ARNOLD:	O.K. Brucie—go to it. (*Stage whisper*) Brucie!
BRUCIE:	(*Slightly off*) What?
ARNOLD:	(*Up slightly*) Say 'hello' to the boss's wife for me!!

[Daws loved the word-play of Howard Cosel and wrote this as a tribute to him. Whether or not you can sound like Cosel does not matter. Enjoy playing with the words and messing with Cogent's mind.]

WORDS
(2 Men or 1 Man and 1 Woman)

HOWARD:	I am Howard Cosell. The name of the program is 'The Howard Cosell Program'...and this morning—not sunny yet, because the dawn is as yet undecided as to the texture it will assume. No...it is not sunny, but clear and crisp and certainly acceptable to my guest and myself.
COGENT:	(*Clears throat loudly*)
HOWARD:	...and it will be my pleasure—as it always is on these clear, crisp mornings...to introduce to you the splendid work of a writer, who's name may be unfamiliar to you.
COGENT:	Tell 'em anyway!
HOWARD:	...and who's subject...in the manuscript he has chosen for presentation on this program...
COGENT:	Tell 'em what it is!
HOWARD:	...and here, I mention the title of his treatise, because treatise, it is!!
COGENT:	It's not a treatise—it's a text-book!!
HOWARD:	It's called 'ECONOMY IN WORD USE.'
COGENT:	Did *you* read it?
HOWARD:	I skimmed through it. I'm a skimmer. I skim.
COGENT:	I can tell! Even the *title* didn't get through to *you*!
HOWARD:	To continue. When I *mention* (and what I'm *about* to mention is *worth* mentioning)—when I *mention* that remembering back to the acclaimed works of Charles Dickens and other worthies of his stature—we must accept the fact that the present is the present and the past is the past.
COGENT:	I'll accept it but let's get movin' on this thing. Tell 'em who I am!

41

HOWARD:	…but it is in the present that we find ourselves today…
COGENT:	Cogent…Fielding Cogent! Tell 'em that my name is Fielding Cogent!!!
HOWARD:	Allow me to introduce our guest on this 'clear'…
COGENT:	(*Up*) Knock it off with that 'clear, crisp' mornin' jazz!!
HOWARD:	The harmlessly eccentric—Mr. Fielding Cogent!
COGENT:	Tell 'em I like to be terse in my writing.
HOWARD:	A commendable admission! You're not averse to terse.
COGENT:	The book I wrote is about terseness.
HOWARD:	Writers of the world, or at least those who are within ear-shot of this program—take heed! There is no sanctuary for the unnecessary word! It will be reviled and spat upon!
COGENT:	I don't think anybody is gonna spit on it. What I'm writin' about here is…if you can say it in a few words, do it for cryin' out loud!
HOWARD:	A daring challenge to the demon of verbosity…who lies waiting for the unwary machinations of the writer's muse!!
COGENT:	(*Sotto*) Just tell 'em to write simple! Let's move it!! (*Shivers*) I turned down Merv Griffin for *this*!! Just write simple!!
HOWARD:	It's not that easy.
COGENT:	It's what my book is all about!! *Read* the damn thing!!
HOWARD:	Don't you realize that those poor, untrained fledglings whose creative wings are now extended for flight…are ill-equipped to heed your advice.
COGENT:	What are you making such a big deal! It's not that tough! Just put it down…and then slash it to ribbons. Cut! Keep it terse! Don't be a fathead!
HOWARD:	(*Chuckles*) I detect—perhaps wrongly, but I could be correct—I detect a subtle jibe at my inclusion of several probably unnecessary words in the various rejoinders I have made to your provocative 'pointing up' of your thesis.
COGENT:	Subtle jibe, my foot! Oh brother! I told my agent that this program would be a loser!
HOWARD:	The sober acceptance of my explanation…and *my* thesis, if you will…has just entered my mind and I find it truly noteworthy.
COGENT:	You got a funny look on your face. Funnier. You gettin' sick?
HOWARD:	It just came to me. I believe that verbosity can prolong life!! What do you think?
COGENT:	I think you're ready for the rubber room!
HOWARD:	I believe that it would be incredibly difficult to expire while

expounding even indifferent prose...and it is a truly unsacreligious comment that I make...when I aver that the 'deity' would have the 'decency' not to be a 'point-killer' and to respect a complex sentence for its entire run!!

COGENT: You lost me!! Let's break it down. In my book I champion the economy of verbiage and...in effect...to 'tell it like it is!!'

HOWARD: Exactly! I couldn't have put it better myself! (*Beat*) Actually, I probably could—but we've run out of time!

[This is a wonderful exercise not only in dialect but in difference in characterization. While both characters are Irish, one is calm and controlled (Paddy) and the other wide-eye and excitable (Sean). Try playing with different body and voice types. For example, Paddy might be a large man with a deep voice, while Sean might be short with a high-pitched voice. This also makes a wonderful audition piece with one actor playing both roles and changing his voice and body posture for each character.]

MARGERY DICKERSON (Irish)
(2 Men or 1 Man, 1 Woman)

PADDY: Why d'ya keep lookin' at me?

SEAN: I thought you might know.

PADDY: Know what?

SEAN: Who she was…an' all about 'er…Margery Dickerson? (*Up*) You've been around here for a while?

PADDY: I have. I was born here.

SEAN: (*Beat*) Well?

PADDY: Well, what?

SEAN: Do ya know about 'er an' all? What happened t'her, I mean.

PADDY: I know as much as anyone else. (*Beat*) Margery Dickerson…fell down one day…and never got up.

SEAN: Never got up?

PADDY: Never got up.

SEAN: Y'mean t'say she fell down an' never got up?

PADDY: Never got up.

SEAN: (*Pause*) Why?

PADDY: She jus' plain didn't want to!

SEAN: (*Beat*) She jus' lay there?

PADDY: She did.

SEAN: On the ground?…or on the floor?

PADDY: On the ground.

SEAN:	Oh, the poor soul! (*Clucks tongue*)
PADDY:	Well, at first, they swept around 'er...sometimes, they would lift up her skirt an' sweep the dirt under it...she never got up. (*Up*) They built a house around 'er...jacked a bed under her an' there she stayed... she never got up.
SEAN:	(*Beat*) She...was a peculiar person!
PADDY:	Why d'ya say that?
SEAN:	(*Taken aback*) Fallin' down an' not gettin' up' (*Beat*} Did she hurt herself?
PADDY:	She never said.
SEAN:	Was she ever asked?
PADDY:	Aye.
SEAN:	...and what'd she say?
PADDY:	Nothin'
SEAN:	Nothin'?...why'd she say...nothin'?
PADDY:	Because she was asleep...an' when she woke up, she grew taciturn. Never surly...always cooperative was Margery Dickerson...but not 'word one' would she utter! She wrote down all her requests in a fine Spenserian hand. (*Up*) They're all bound now and kept in the museum by the main road's turnin'...(*Up*) You could go see 'em if you'd like!
SEAN:	(*Beat*) So they...so they built a house around 'er?
PADDY:	Not really a house...well, it was a wee house...only one room. (*Up*) There was only her, y'see.
SEAN:	But how did she live? I mean...who took care of 'er?
PADDY:	The townspeople. They drew lots every day...the loser, would look after Margery Dickerson's needs.
SEAN:	On that particular day?
PADDY:	On that particular day, aye. She would be fed what she desired.
SEAN:	(*Beat*)...and what was that?
PADDY:	It was always the same...barley cereal, with great chunks of fat...slightly browned in the skillet...an' a wee drop t'wash it down!
SEAN:	That was her way of life, then?
PADDY:	It was, indeed.
SEAN:	(*Pause*) It is a strange tale.
PADDY:	She was a strange woman, was Margery Dickerson.
SEAN:	(*Concerned*) I wish I had known 'er...I would have been able to talk some sense into 'er! (*Up*) I woulda made her get up and

	become part of the world again!
PADDY:	Others tried…they failed.
SEAN:	(*Beat*) Why?
PADDY:	(*Quickly*) She jus' plain didn't wanna get up…it was as simple as that! She lived in that wee house until the day she died.
SEAN:	It were a tragedy, pure! Niver, to my sartain knowledge has there ever been one the like of it. (*Pause*) Margery Dickerson lived there till the day she died?
PADDY:	She did.
SEAN:	How old was she when she died?
PADDY:	Ninety-two.
SEAN:	Ninety-two!! The saints be praised! Ninety-two!
PADDY:	Well, she was Old.
SEAN:	Poor lost creature! (*Pause*) How old was she when she fell down?
PADDY:	Ninety-two.
SEAN:	{*Up*) Ninety-two!
PADDY:	Well, she died three weeks later.
SEAN:	Three weeks! But you made it sound as if she spent her whole great long life there – lyin' in a bed, in a one-room house! Whatta ya call this ramblin' argosy of words, that're now pointless and inane!??
PADDY:	I call it…conversation.

[This is a scene from one of Daws' Sherlock Holmes radio plays. Playing Holmes is a test for any actor since most audiences will have preconceived notions of what he should look and sound like. Try to play him your own way, not as an imitation of Basil Rathbone.]

MR. DALRYMPLE
(2 Men)

DALRYMPLE: You must excuse the dust, and what appears to be...but is not...disorganized clutter. It is, indeed, organized clutter. It is my clutter. I know the secrets it contains. (*Chuckle*) I am jealous and possessive of a clutter no one covets.

HOLMES: I appreciate the trouble you're going to, Mr. Dalrymple.

DALRYMPLE: That is the purpose of my files, my good sir! If your young lady is in them, she'll not get away from me. I know nothing of her strength and spirit...and she may fight and scratch, but I'll find her, make no mistake! (*Beat*) Fraser, y'say?

HOLMES: Mary Fraser. She left Adelaide with her maid... bound for England in 1895...on The Rock of Gibraltar.

DALRYMPLE: (*Tuneless humming*) The Rock of Gibraltar... passenger list...(*Up*) Here we are...the cast of characters...the players themselves! Dubish. Raoul Dubish...traveling with his maiden Aunt Deborah. Raoul Dubish (*Light chuckle*) Deborah Dubish! (*Light chuckle*) Ah, here's another...

HOLMES: It's in the 'F's, Mr. Dalrymple — Fraser. Mary Fraser.

DALRYMPLE: I'm amused by names. When I get into my files, I look for amusement as well as expediency. (*Change*) Here's one—Vincent Carlos Eggleminger and his Madrigal Singers. (*Beat*) Eggleminger! (*Light chuckle*) What's a Madrigal, I wonder? Oh well, it's not amusing.

HOLMES: (*Pointedly*) Fraser.

DALRYMPLE: (*Tuneless humming*) Ah, here it is! Mary Fraser! Don't try to get away, my dear—thumb and forefinger have got you fast. Mary Fraser, travelin' with her maid, Theresa Rogers.

HOLMES: That's the one! What does it say about the ship's officers? Who they were then—who they are now. (*Up*) The same?

DALRYMPLE: At this point, they would be somewhere south of the Suez Canal on the way to Australia…

HOLMES: (*Slight annoyance*) The same officers?

DALRYMPLE: The same, yes…except…

HOLMES: Except?

DALRYMPLE: Except for Jack Crocker. He was recently made a captain. He'll take charge of a newly commissioned ship…the Bass Rock…

HOLMES: …sailing when?

DALRYMPLE: Sailing in two days time. (*Slight chuckle*) Crocker. (*Chuckle*) That's an amusin' name, too!

HOLMES: Somewhere on there…does it say where Crocker lives in England?

DALRYMPLE: …lives…Crocker… (*Light chuckle*) England… (*Beat—up*) Sydenham…(*Pronounced 'Syd'n'm'*)

HOLMES: (*Thoughtful*) Sydenham.

DALRYMPLE: He'll be in later this mornin'—you could speak to him.

HOLMES: Not necessary. What can you tell me about him?

DALRYMPLE: Crocker. (*Light chuckle*) Amusin'…Nice young chap. Good man on ship…reliable, don't you know? But he's a bit of a wild one on shore. Lives life to the full, you might say. Everybody likes him. I like him. (*Light chuckle*) Crocker. (*Light chuckle*)

HOLMES: You've been most thorough, Mr. Dalrymple.

DALRYMPLE: It's been my pleasure to have found your young lady, Mr…

HOLMES: Holmes. Sherlock Holmes.

DALRYMPLE: (*Perks up*) Sherlock. (*Up*) Sherlock! (*Light chuckle*)

HOLMES: Amusing? (*Beat—pointed*) What's your first name, Mr. Dalrymple?

DALRYMPLE: Lafcadio.

HOLMES: Lafcadio. Lafcadio Dalrymple.

HOLMES: (*Laugh*)

DALRYMPLE: (*Miffed*) What's amusin' about my name? (*Pause—Light chuckle*) Oh, I see!

BOTH: (*Laugh*)

[Daws loved arguments of semantics. Take special note of the italicized words in this script and emphasize them while at the same time reacting naturally to how your partner delivers her lines.]

POLLY AND ASPERSION
(The Cast)
(2 Women)

AUNT:	To begin with…because I think the beginning is the best part of the discussion…what is your little name?
POLLY:	You know my name.
AUNT:	(*Stresses*) Your *little* name.
POLLY:	You know my '*little*' name, Great-Aunt Aspersion!
AUNT:	(*Stresses*) *That*…is *my* name! Great-Aunt Aspersion is *my* name. It is not *your* name! Your '*little*' name, I might add.
POLLY:	You just did!
AUNT:	Your '*little*' name sounds nothing like Great-Aunt Aspersion. Never has! Never will!
POLLY:	Then why did you ask me what my name was…
AUNT:	(*Quick*) Your *little* name…
POLLY:	Then why did you ask me what my *little* name was?…if you already knew.
AUNT:	I knew…That's true…But I forgot.
POLLY:	You forgot my *name*. (*Quickly*) My '*little*' name?
AUNT:	Yes.
POLLY:	…but everyone tells *me* that you tell *them* that I'm your *favorite* niece!…and now you tell me that you didn't remember my name.
BOTH:	'*Little*' name!!
AUNT:	I remember my 'un-favorite' nieces.
POLLY:	Why?
AUNT:	So I won't bother to send them presents.
POLLY:	(*Thinks*)…but you haven't sent me any presents lately.

AUNT:	Of course not!…and there's a reason for that!
POLLY:	A good reason?
AUNT:	A 'Jim Dandy' reason.
POLLY:	What is the reason?
AUNT:	A 'Jim Dandy!'
POLLY:	That's not what I mean! What I mean is…'what is the *Jim Dandy* reason?'
AUNT:	I'm stingy.
POLLY:	You're stingy?
AUNT:	'Slow with a buck!' (*Up*) Oh Darling niece, you're the apple of my good eye! My being stingy has nothing to do with the great affection I feel for you! (*Dramatic pause*} But…I must qualify priorities.
POLLY:	I've heard of people who did that. I didn't know that *you* did that.
AUNT:	We're a select group. In the Yellow Pages we're listed as 'Priority Qualifiers.' There's going to be a television special about us and our activities…
POLLY:	Will it be in the TV Guide?
AUNT:	*It better be! It just better be!! Or else!!*
POLLY:	(*Concerned*) Your nostrils are flaring!
AUNT:	They'd *better* be! I'm in a 'nostril flaring' mood today!
POLLY:	Tell me some more about 'priorities!' This is exciting!
AUNT:	I don't want to frighten you…but there are times when purchasing an extra cinnamon bun to enjoy with my morning Dr. Pepper…
POLLY:	*I* like Dr. Pepper…!!
AUNT:	It's *great*! Do you like cinnamon buns?
POLLY:	They're O.K.
AUNT:	(*Loud*) *They're great*!!
POLLY:	If we have some, sometime…you can have mine.
AUNT:	*Great*! I'll remember that! Cinnamon buns are *great*!
POLLY:	What has this got to do with your being stingy?
AUNT:	I was just gonna ask you why you didn't ask me that!
POLLY:	I already did. You're too late. What *has* this got to do with your being stingy?
AUNT:	As I said before…'There are times when purchasing an extra cinnamon bun to enjoy with my morning DR. PEPPER…is a strong enough temptation to put *you*…and my great love for you…completely out of my mind.'

POLLY:	Sometimes you confuse me, Aunt Aspersion.
AUNT:	*No!*...you confuse *me*! My knowledge is greater than yours...and I am not as easily confused. I put things in their proper perspective.
POLLY:	Because you're stingy? Be fair about this. Don't you think that remembering my name...my '*little*' name should be in your 'proper perspective?'
AUNT:	Yes, I do. I'll make a note of it.
POLLY:	When? Sometimes you're very vague.
AUNT:	When I find my *pencil*.
POLLY:	You can use *my* pencil.
AUNT:	I like *my* pencil better. It's got a sharp point.
POLLY:	*My* pencil has a sharp point!
AUNT:	My pencil has an *eraser*.
POLLY:	*My* pencil has an eraser!
AUNT:	(*Long pause*) No.
POLLY:	Why not?
AUNT:	I like my pencil better. We go way back.
POLLY:	But you *lost* it. How could you *lose* something you *liked* so much?
AUNT:	I didn't like it *that* much. It was a good pencil as pencils went...and it *did*...but I can live without it.
POLLY:	(*Pause*) Aunt Aspersion...
AUNT:	Yes, Polly.
POLLY:	*Polly*!! That's my name! You remembered my name!
AUNT:	Your '*little*' name.
POLLY:	Why do you keep calling it my '*little*' name?
AUNT:	Because 'Polly' means '*little*' in Greek.
POLLY:	But my ancestors came from Denmark...and 'Polly' in Danish means 'Banana squash.' A banana squash isn't '*little*.' A banana squash is *big*. It's *big*, Aunt Aspersion!
AUNT:	Then what's your 'big' name?
POLLY:	Polly.
AUNT:	Fine. That's just fine. I'm going to lie down now.
POLLY:	But what about the discussion? You said we were going to have a discussion!!
AUNT:	We just had it.
POLLY:	Now what'll *I* do?
AUNT:	Go look for my pencil.

[This is among the most difficult of all Daws' dialogues because at first glance it appears to be a straight-forward dialogue, until you realize one of the characters is a puppet. The challenge here is to play it as natural as possible and not give away the gimmick until the very end. Daws used to say, "Even if you are playing a cartoon dog or a bear, you play him as if he were real flesh and blood."]

RELATING
(2 Men or 2 Women)

GUTSY: I gotta get my act together, Red......I gotta start relating to people. You know what I mean?

RED: Not exactly. What're you getting at, Gutsy?

GUTSY: I just write about people 'relating.'

RED: That's because it's what you do.....I think you relate.

GUTSY: But I *only* do it on paper. (*New thought*) Do I ever relate to you? It's always been my intention.

RED: I never thought about it. Do I relate to you?

GUTSY: Sure. You tell me things about yourself...about people you know...about things that happened. So cleverly.

RED: And you don't do that?

GUTSY: Not as good as you. I always have to embellish my thoughts – exaggerate – make it sound more important than it is.

RED: I like it when you do that. It's dramatic. It sounds just like a story and you're just telling it to me. It's like 'my' story. If you tell the same thing to somebody else it would be 'different'...it would be 'their story.'

GUTSY: You've got me figured out. You make my ego wince.

RED: I like to be with you. It's where I belong.

GUTSY: Doesn't it bother you? My shortcomings?

RED: No. To me, they're 'tall-comings.' (*Giggle*)

GUTSY: I can never tell something exactly as it happened. I'm always afraid it won't be interesting enough to hold someone's attention...that they'll yawn...or start looking at the wallpaper.

RED: You shouldn't feel that way.

GUTSY:	I talk fast so they won't walk away before I'm finished.
RED:	I never think about things like this. I just talk.
GUTSY:	And you do it good.
RED:	How do you mean…'good?'
GUTSY:	You don't push – you just lay out what you've got to say and people listen and then they say something which ties in with what you've said. You have a dialogue.
RED:	We're having a dialogue right now.
GUTSY:	Really?
RED:	Sure. (*Change of thought*) The trouble with you, is…. maybe I shouldn't say this.
GUTSY:	Sure you should! What *is* the trouble with me?
RED:	You fabricate reality – you twist it…you shape it. You 'invent' reality and the 'play of ideas' which are directed only by you. They're in your head, Gutsy – in your head. You play both parts. You do.
GUTSY:	That's right! You've hit it!
RED:	That puts you in control.
GUTSY:	…and I'm not in control when I'm with a real person, right?
RED:	Right. Some people are intimidated when they're with you because they know that you're a writer and what they say might be boring to you.
GUTSY:	No, I like it when people talk to me and tell me things about themselves.
RED:	You should do the same thing with them. It's easy.
GUTSY:	But here's the thing, Red…I'm always looking for a 'hook' to what I'm saying .. a sort of a joke finish. I want to be entertaining. I can't just *say* something.
RED:	You're just 'saying something' now.
GUTSY:	That's because you're my best friend. I feel completely comfortable with you.
RED:	I feel comfortable with you. I never think about the things you've been driving yourself crazy thinking about.
GUTSY:	I make too much out of things, don't I, Red?
RED:	You always have. That's why your name's 'Gutsy.' You're not afraid to go out on a limb. You know that the limb won't break if you're on it. Everything will work out.
GUTSY:	And everything does. I did and I do what I set out to do… I write about the things that are in my head.

RED:	I can't do that.
GUTSY:	But you have friends – everybody loves you.
RED:	I can't take all the credit for that. It's because I'm a puppet.
GUTSY:	I know.
RED:	Whatever I am, came from you. (*Beat*) Incidentally, your hand is cold.

[A different spin on the "Margery Dickerson" tale, told in the style of one of Daws' favorites: the great Jewish storyteller Myron Cohen.]

SYLVIA SILVERMAN (Jewish)
(1 Man, 2 Woman or 2 Men, 1 Woman)

TWO:	(*Up*) Hey, Rose! It's over here with the toasted bagel!
ROSE:	(*Comes on*) It's coming! (*Beat*) You don't like the service?
TWO:	The Army I could put up with…this place, I donno.
ROSE:	You never take my meaning.
TWO:	From you, I'll take anything I can get. How about my bagel?
ROSE:	(*Going off*) I'm sending it United Parcel…it'll save me…some aggravation!!
ONE:	Anybody at this table?
TWO:	I'm at this table.
ONE:	Besides you.
TWO:	It's possible. You wanna sit?
ONE:	I'll sit
TWO:	So sit. (*Calls*) Hey, Rose! Where's the bagel?
ROSE:	(*Comes on*) Here's your bagel. (*Beat*) It's toasted.
TWO:	I asked for it, toasted!
ROSE:	(*Lays it out*) In spite of that!! (*Beat*) Inside, I can't help it—I gotta remain a warm person.
TWO:	Rose, look on the dark side already…if I didn't come in here, your ulcer would heal…
ROSE:	(*Up*) What ulcer!
TWO:	You don't have an ulcer?
ROSE:	No.
TWO:	How d'ya like that?!! I'm over-doin' the jolly bit!! (*Beat*) What're you standing?

ROSE:	Pay me for the bagel…I'm going off in five minutes.
TWO:	I can't wait for the count-down…and listen, Rose, on a single bagel, I wouldn't leave a tip! After four bagels, I'll leave a tip, don' worry about it! (*Up*) You keep track!
ROSE:	Huh?
TWO:	Why should *I* keep track? Keep books on your own bagels! (*Calls*) You got my permission to be a nudge! (*Down}* A detail man I'm not.
ONE:	(*Up*) Rose! You'll bring me a celery tonic, I'll appreciate it!!
TWO:	(*Tongue*) Tsk, tsk, tsk, tsk!
ONE:	Why you're tiss ticking? You don' like the bagel?
TWO:	(*Down*) Such a thing should happen! (*Tongue clucking*)
ONE:	An accident?
TWO:	(*Up*) You…call it an accident!!
ONE:	I'm asking! What happened already?
TWO:	Sylvia Silverman…fell down one day…and she never got up.
ONE:	Never got up?
TWO:	Never got up.
ONE:	She fell down and she never got up…she was meshugga?
TWO:	(*Shrugs*) She jus' din' wanna get up—it bothers you?
ONE:	She jus' lay dere?
TWO:	You got it!
ONE:	On the ground? Or on the floor?
TWO:	On the ground.
ONE:	Oh boy!!
TWO:	See, what they did, first, they swept around her. Sometimes, they would lift up her skirt and sweep the dirt under it…
ONE:	Oh boy!
TWO:	She never got up. What they did, they built a house around her…jacked a bed under her…an' she lived there. She never got up.
ONE:	(*Beat*) She…was a peculiar type lady!
TWO:	Why you say that?
ONE:	Fallin' down…an' not gettin' up.
TWO:	(*Shrugs*) You got a point.
ONE:	(*Beat*) Did she hurt herself?
TWO:	She din' say.

ONE: Did anybody ask her?

TWO: Certainly!

ONE: So what'd she say?

TWO: Nuttin'.

ONE: Nuttin'?

TWO: Nuttin'!—not a word—not a syllable.

ONE: (*Up*) Not even a whimper?

TWO: (*Shrugs*) Maybe a whimper. (*Beat*) She was asleep. When she woke up, she wouldn't talk…on Johnny Carson's, she'd never get!!

ONE: (*Thinks*) So…so they built a house around her?

TWO: What house? It was a dinky…a little nuttin' of a house. One lousy room…who needed more? There was only Sylvia!

ONE: How did Sylvia live? Who took care of her?

TWO: Next door—across the street—there were people there. Every day, without fail…they would draw lots. (*Throw-away*) The loser would take care of Sylvia… whatever Sylvia wanted, she would get.

ONE: So?

TWO: So…what?

ONE: So what'd she get?

TWO: It was always the same,…her favorite! On a matzo, was a great glob schmaltz…an' a celery tonic to wash it down!

ONE: (*Clucks—yells*) Hey, Rose! Where's with my celery tonic, already!! (*Down—heart-felt*) So that's how it was with Sylvia?

TWO: (*Up*) You're not listening? You want an instant replay?

ONE: I'm the one! I should have known Sylvia. I would've been able to talk some sense into her. (*Yells*) I would've made her get up and be part of the world again!!

TWO: (*Up*) Don't holler!! (*Shrugs*) Others tried. Didn't work. She din' wanna get up, it was as simple as that. Sylvia Silverman lived in that dinky house until the day she died!

ONE: How old was Sylvia when she died?

TWO: Ninety-two.

ONE: Ninety-two! Oy!! Ninety-two!!

TWO: (*Throw-away*) If you gotta die, ninety-two, ain't bad!

ONE: How old was Sylvia when she fell down?

TWO: Ninety-two.

ONE: (*Yells*) NINETY-TWO!!!!

TWO:	Don't holler! She died three weeks later.
ONE:	Three weeks?!! Draykup wit the shmegegge!! You made it sound like she spent her whole long life there—livin' in a dinky…in a one room house!! So why'd you give me, with all those words!!!
TWO:	(*Spreads hands*) Schlemiel!! Why not!?? It goes nice with a nosh!!

MESHUGGA (Rhyme with 'Paducah'—means CRAZY)

MATZOH {Rhyme with 'lotsa'—means UNLEAVENED BREAD)

SCHMALTZ (means CHICKEN FAT)

DRAYKUP (Rhyme with 'gray pup'—means SOMEONE WHO CONFUSES YOU)

SHMEGEGGE (Rhyme with 'the peggy'—means BALONEY—NONSENSE)

SCHLEMIEL (Rhyme with 'reveal'—means A FALL GUY—A BORN LOSER)

[This is a very intimate piece and the audience should feel as if they are eavesdropping on a real married couple, learning something new about each other. It should be played very relaxed and quiet. There is no need to follow the script word-for-word. Try repeating a word or phrase, stumbling on a line, laughing in an unusual place, yawning through a line, etc.]

FORGET METAPHOR...
WHATTA YOU MEAN?
(1 Man, 1 Woman)

DENNIS:	You finally got up, huh?
BRENDA:	I didn't sleep good last night. This morning I was sleepy so I slept.
DENNIS:	I'm not gonna write that down. I can remember it.
BRENDA:	Oh stop!!
DENNIS:	Not till the light in your eyes changes.
BRENDA:	You got up early?
DENNIS:	God washed the car last night. It's streaky, as usual.
BRENDA:	It rained.
DENNIS:	That isn't what I said.
BRENDA:	Why can't you just say things right out—just make a statement? 'God washed the car last night!' Oh, my God!
DENNIS:	Watch your tone, Brenda. Show a little respect, I mean, when you get your car washed for nothing you should show a little respect.
BRENDA:	What is your point? Why do you always have to embroider?
DENNIS:	Why not embroider? You want me to be...dull?
BRENDA:	I don't embroider. Am I dull?
DENNIS:	Pretty dull, yeh. Most people are dull. They play everything too close to the vest...or in your case, brassiere.
BRENDA:	But you never stop—that little mind of yours is always working over-time, trying to be clever.
DENNIS:	Trying?

BRENDA:	Sometimes you *are* clever…mostly, you're annoying. You have to be 'on' all the time. You're like a puppy-dog and you're not particular about whose lap you're on.
DENNIS:	You'd like it better if I just said, 'It rained last night?'
BRENDA:	It's not a question of liking it—its minimally informational. I would have discovered that fact myself as soon as I looked out the window.
DENNIS:	What if you didn't look out the window?
BRENDA:	Oh stop! Will you stoppp!
DENNIS:	What if…because of your slovenly nature, the window had gotten layered over with the accumulation of dust, dirt and grime? What if…'*that*?' What *if*!
BRENDA:	I'm going out. (*Change*) Dennis, when we got married, I knew what you were like…'then'…but I thought there would be a metamorphosis…
DENNIS:	'Simple Simon met-a-morphosis going to the…'
BRENDA:	You insist on just being the cocoon…you're happy being the cocoon! But I know that somewhere inside—if I can wait long enough—there's a little worm, fighting to get out.
DENNIS:	I always wondered what it was that made me fall in love with you—and now I know!
BRENDA:	What?
DENNIS:	I'm nuts! Whacko! I got cream-of-wheat in my skull!!
BRENDA:	Whatta you think made me fall in love with *you*?
DENNIS:	There you go! Always using sex as a crutch! You never could keep your hands offa me…bobby-pinning my cow-lick, brushing off lint.
BRENDA:	You know why I fell in love with you?
DENNIS:	I just told you.
BRENDA:	I want a second opinion and I've got it. I fell in love with you because…(*Cries*)
DENNIS:	Awwwww! whatsamatter, Brenda? Don't cry!
BRENDA:	I don't *know* why I fell in love with you. I just did! You are nuts and whacko and you do have cream-of-wheat in your skull…but I can't help loving you!
DENNIS:	A spell has been cast over you! You are powerless! Do I have an aquiline nose?
BRENDA:	No.
DENNIS:	A strong jaw?

BRENDA: No.

DENNIS: Is there any distinguishing feature about me that makes me unique?

BRENDA: No.

DENNIS: How about sex appeal?

BRENDA: I think so.

DENNIS: You *think* so?

BRENDA: You're attractive.

DENNIS: That's all?

BRENDA: That should be enough. (*Change*) How long have we been married?

DENNIS: You're complaining?

BRENDA: Just fact-finding. How long?

DENNIS: Six years.

BRENDA: Do you still love me?

DENNIS: Of course!

BRENDA: Do I still love you?

DENNIS: Of course!

BRENDA: How can you be so sure?

DENNIS: Conceit! I can't imagine you're not loving me, I'm so...special.

BRENDA: Then it's decided...we love each other. (*Change*) But why do you always have to 'show-off?'

DENNIS: Whatta you mean 'show-off?'

BRENDA: With all of your metaphor...you can't ever say anything straight out...why do you always have to indulge in hyperbole?

DENNIS: I don't want you to think me ordinary. I like to say things with a twist...a switch—I want to be like no one you've ever known...an original...you never know what I'm gonna come up with!!

BRENDA: It doesn't matter.

DENNIS: It doesn't?

BRENDA: It's never mattered—*that* doesn't matter.

DENNIS: I can just be an ordinary run-of-the-mill slob and you'd still like me?

BRENDA: You *are* an ordinary run-of-the-mill slob and I *do* like you.

DENNIS: Then why did I try so hard to impress you all these years?

BRENDA: Why? Why, Dennis? You loved me. I loved you.

DENNIS: You love me regardless of everything?

BRENDA:	Everything.
DENNIS:	I don't have to dazzle you with my footwork? Any work?
BRENDA:	No.
DENNIS:	Wow!
BRENDA:	Chemistry, Dennis—just chemistry. No intellectualizing...no metaphor—no fancy-fancy.
DENNIS:	It's too easy. I don't deserve having your love that easy!
BRENDA:	Yes, you do.
DENNIS:	Then my post-graduate course in smart-ass rejoinders was to no avail?
BRENDA:	No avail.
DENNIS:	You just love me?
BRENDA:	I just love you.
DENNIS:	I can just be dull and mundane and boring...and insufferable?
BRENDA:	If you want.
DENNIS:	How about you?
BRENDA:	I can be dull and boring and insufferable too.
DENNIS:	You can and you are—but it doesn't matter. What you said is right—we love each other just because we love each other.
BRENDA:	A strong philosophical basis.
DENNIS:	I won't say things like 'God washed the car last night.' I'll just say—it rained last night.
BRENDA:	I'll know what you mean. You don't have to clothe everything you say in metaphor.
DENNIS:	I'll just be a dull bastard—straight-out—no individuality...I could be just a guy coming around the corner...right?
BRENDA:	Right.
DENNIS:	You prefer that?
BRENDA:	If it's you...I don't want you to keep walking the fence...showing off.
DENNIS:	O.K. (*Change*) God washed the car last night.
BRENDA:	Streaky, as usual?
DENNIS:	Streaky. (*Change*) Do you have to go out this morning?
BRENDA:	No.
DENNIS:	Then don't.
BRENDA:	I won't.
DENNIS:	More coffee?

[When playing this script, remember the characters do not know each other at first. There is an awkwardness to the early lines that slowly gives way to more comfortable language as the two people develop a rapport.]

EVERY DOG HAS 'HER' DAY!
(1 Man, 1 Woman)

MARGARET:	(*On the telephone*) Hello, Mother?…Margaret. Listen, about this afternoon…all I know is that he's on his way right now (should be here any minute). (*Hurried*) Mother, I don't know if he's good-looking! (What's that got to do with anything? He's not a date!) Look, I'm using the hand-phone out on the front porch…so when I see him coming I can hang up. (*Sigh*) Mother…all I know is that Linda is sending him over to…meet me. He's looking for a copy-writing job at our agency. He's new in town and who knows what 'crazy Linda' is up too!! (*Change*) I see someone coming up to the house. (*Up*) I think it's him! (*Quick*) G'bye!
LEW:	Hi. I was just looking to see if this was the right address. I'm Lew Tarkman.
MARGARET:	I'm sure it's the right address.
LEW:	I'm Lew Tarkman.
MARGARET:	I know.
LEW:	I'm looking for some 'dog'…name of Margaret. Anyone named Margaret live here?
MARGARET:	(*Flatly*) My name is Margaret.
LEW:	(*Beat*) *You* live here?
MARGARET:	I live here. (*Up*) Mr. Tarkman…
LEW:	Incidentally, I just noticed…you're not a 'dog!'
MARGARET:	Who said I *was* a dog?
LEW:	Not me! Hell no! It was Linda!
MARGARET:	Linda?
LEW:	Yeh, Linda…with a last name *nobody* remembers!
MARGARET:	You mean Linda *Brown*?

LEW:	(*Impressed*) Yeh, Brown! You remembered it, right off!
MARGARET:	Linda said I was a 'dog?'
LEW:	Yeh. She said: 'I wancha to go see this friend of mine…
MARGARET:	Friend? She used the word…'friend?'
LEW:	(*Goes on*)…friend of mine, name's Margaret. She's a 'dog', but her family's got plenty of money…"
MARGARET:	(*Playing*) Listen, Mr. Tarkman…I was prepared to meet you as Linda 'apparently' suggested…but your opening gambit is losing you a lot of points. (*Change*) Incidentally, just what is your point?
LEW:	My opening 'overture' was clumsy, I admit…but let me continue. Linda said: 'Margaret's *mother* runs an Advertising Agency and it might do you some good to go out with her…'
MARGARET:	(*Up*)…with my *mother*?
LEW:	Sorry, no! I mean, 'go out with you!' Linda said…
MARGARET:	I'm getting very tired of Linda!
LEW:	Linda said…'Margaret is her mother's copy-chief and she might be just the catalyst for your career…'
MARGARET:	(*Tongue-in-cheek*) Mr. Tarkman, we're standing outside…
LEW:	Both of us, yeh.
MARGARET:	…and, if you were going to say something about my opening any doors for you…forget it! (*Phony dramatics*) Incidentally, that breeze you just felt was a *door*…slamming!
LEW:	(*Innocent*) What's up? What's up? What's up? Did I say something wrong?
MARGARET:	I think you did. You said that I was a 'dog!' (*Spaced*) You…said… that!
LEW:	Misnomer! That's a misnomer! *Linda* said you were a 'dog!'
MARGARET:	If 'our' friend, Linda, said I was a 'dog,' then why'd you come over here?
LEW:	('*Sincere*') I thought you might be able to help me! (*Switch*) If you didn't bite me first!
MARGARET:	(*Suppressed giggle*) I should have!
LEW:	(*Innocent*) And who could blame you? (*Change*) Look, Margaret…I gotta tell you something about myself. I 'use' people…I try to throw 'em off guard.
MARGARET:	You tried to 'use' me? I don't care what your reasons were…I just don't like it!
LEW:	One reason! I'll give you just one reason! I've been bustin' a gut tryin' to get me an agency job in this town. At this point, I

wouldn't mind gettin' some help from a 'dog.'

MARGARET: Well, you aren't getting any.

LEW: But I'd rather get some help from a smooth chick like you.

MARGARET: You know what 'this smooth chick' thinks? This 'smooth chick' thinks *you're* a dog!!

LEW: *Au contraire*!! Nix. You don't call 'men' dogs!...only women. (*Quickly*) I can't tell you what men are 'called,' because it would be too gross for your tiny ears! (*Change*)...an' you wanna know something?

MARGARET: What?

LEW: Linda didn't call you a 'dog.' Actually, Linda said some nice things about you.

MARGARET: What were they?

LEW: (*Beat*) I forget. (*Up*) Who could remember all those superlatives?

MARGARET: (*Likes him*) I'll tell you one thing, Lew Tarkman...you're off the beaten-path. You made your pitch some 'inside-out' way. You're an original...

LEW: (*Up*) Don't stop!

MARGARET: ...and I think you've made your 'point.' (*Change*) Come down to the agency tomorrow. I'll introduce you to my mother.

LEW: What a neat lady!!

MARGARET: My mother?

LEW: No...you.

MARGARET: What about my mother?

LEW: I'll give you an evaluation after I meet her. I go by the book.

MARGARET: (*Laughs*) You're crazy, Lew...but I like your style. You belong in advertising.

LEW: (*Humble*) You mean I've got the job.

MARGARET: I mean that you've got an 'interview' with my mother tomorrow morning.

LEW: This is a smart move on your part. You'll be glad you helped me...you lucky dog!! (*Both laugh*)

[This is one of Daws' "flirt" pieces. It is a look at how people act when they first meet in a public place. It can be played as if what they are telling each other is true or as if one or the other (or both) is spinning yarn.]

A SAD STORY
(1 Man, 1 Woman)

REYNOLDS:	Mind if I sit down here?
SAD:	Would you mind if I mind?
REYNOLDS:	Yes.
SAD:	I don't mind.
REYNOLDS:	Thanks. (*Beat*) This is the pits! This cocktail party is the worst I've ever suffered through.
SAD:	Why did you come?
REYNOLDS:	I was bored.
SAD:	Are you still bored?
REYNOLDS:	Not now. You're the only good thing about it. I'm glad I ran into you.
SAD:	You didn't honk.
REYNOLDS:	Huh?
SAD:	I said 'You didn't honk.' I'm glad I ran into you.
REYNOLDS:	'You' didn't honk.
SAD:	I don't like second-hand jokes.
REYNOLDS:	Was it a joke?
SAD:	I think so.
REYNOLDS:	Did anyone laugh?
SAD:	No.
REYNOLDS:	Then maybe it wasn't a joke after all. (*Beat*)…You wanna dance?
SAD:	There's no dance floor.
REYNOLDS:	In spite of that. If you'd like to dance—we'll dance.
SAD:	On the carpet?

REYNOLDS:	It's not impossible.
SAD:	I don't wanna dance.
REYNOLDS:	(*Change*) Incidentally, my name's Reynolds—what's yours?
SAD:	It's Sad.
REYNOLDS:	Your name is 'Sad'—what's sad about it?
SAD:	My 'for real name' is Sad.
REYNOLDS:	What's your last name—'commentary?'
SAD:	(*Giggles*) No, but that'd be a good one!
REYNOLDS:	I've never known anyone named 'Sad.'
SAD:	You just *barely know me*. (*Tells the story*) See…my folks named me Sad. Not after any saint…I don't think.
REYNOLDS:	I never heard of a saint named 'Sad.'
SAD:	…but I guess lots of saints *were* sad.
REYNOLDS:	I'll check it out on my computer.
SAD:	Never mind…it's not important…I'm not even a Catholic. My folks just came up with nutty names like that.
REYNOLDS:	I don't know where the hell this is going—but I think you've brought back the art of conversation.
SAD:	I'm glad. We had a cat once, named 'God Almighty.' (*Giggles*) I think it embarrassed him…so I called him 'Goddy.'
REYNOLDS:	…it sort of changed the connotation, right?
SAD:	Right.
REYNOLDS:	…and your folks called you 'Sad.'
SAD:	(*Rambles on*) When I was a baby, I had this big, wide-eyed, serious expression on my face when I was lying in my crib…when I was in the hospital I mean. We never had a crib at home…so my folks just put me in this big old bed, with 'things on the side' so I wouldn't fall out.
REYNOLDS:	Good.
SAD:	…and my folks, and my *older brother, Duck*…seemed to think of it at the same precise moment!
REYNOLDS:	Duck?
SAD:	…and they all said 'Let's call her 'Sad!' So my name is Sad! That's the exegesis.
REYNOLDS:	(*Chuckles*) And your brother's name is 'Duck?' (*Up*) *Exegesis*?
SAD:	It means 'explanation.'
REYNOLDS:	Let's get back to your brother.

SAD:	…when they brought him home and he was in his crib, he used to push his lips out like this (*Does so*) so he looked like a baby duck. (*Holds lips out*)
REYNOLDS:	(*Up*) Wait a minute!
SAD:	(*Holds lips out*) I'm not hinting for a kiss—I'm just showing you how he did with his lips in his crib.
REYNOLDS:	Wait a minute! How'd you know this?
SAD:	Huh?
REYNOLDS:	You said your brother was 'older' than you.
SAD:	He was.
REYNOLDS:	Then how'd you know?
SAD:	My folks told me about it.
REYNOLDS:	So there *was* a crib in your house after all. Whatever became of it?
SAD:	(*Awed*) It never dawned on me! My folks probably sold it—or gave it away—or maybe they didn't think they'd need it again.
REYNOLDS:	But they did!
SAD:	(*Sexy*) Are you glad?
REYNOLDS:	Yeh, Sad—I'm glad. (*Change*) There's no music, but let's go dance on the carpet.
SAD:	(*Giggles*) We can hum!!

[As with most of his scripts, Daws gave very little direction and asked the actors to find the characters and their relationship to each other themselves. The question to ask here is: who is manipulating whom? Try it both ways and see what develops.]

POOCHIE SORTS IT OUT
(1 Man, 1 Woman)

DERMOT: ...it's not clear to me at all, Poochie...you've made all these plans and I'm expected to go along with them...but why?

POOCHIE: You just are.

DERMOT: Why wasn't I consulted? It *is* my money that's making your trip possible.

POOCHIE: It didn't have to be. You insisted. You said—'I'll lay out the cash—you come up with the itinerary.' Well, I came up with the itinerary.

DERMOT: You're going to Egypt? New Zealand? The continent?

POOCHIE: Why not? You've got plenty of money. I've got plenty of time. Those are the places I wanna see.

DERMOT: How long will you be gone?

POOCHIE: Two or three years...who knows? What difference does it make? Uncle Dermot—when you got custody of me, you said you'd give me anything I wanted...and so far, you have...The things I wanted that were tactile—that I could feel—baked enamel I could run my hand over...God knows how much my Mercedes two-seater set you back...

DERMOT: Fifty-seven thousand which included the extras you wanted.

POOCHIE: Then *you* and God knows! In the last Olympics I finished first in the high-hurdles and broad jump—gold medals...You flipped out...made you proud, didn't I? (*Change*) Now that I've graduated from the University...and I'm still only eighteen—and I've got that Fellowship waiting for me at Duke...whenever I want it...why are you so damned upset at my taking off for a few years? I'm young...I want 'out' now...I wanna 'go!' Can't you understand that?

DERMOT: Why didn't we talk about it? I could have shifted things around...made some adjustments...I could have made some plans too! I could go with you!

POOCHIE: I don't want you to go with me! I don't want anyone to go with me! I want to go! Me! I want to get the hell out of here. I'm too damn smart! I can have it all too fast…and when I get it, what is it? It's tactile…I can feel it…I wanna find something ephemeral…something without substance—something that I can't see—something that may not even be there as far as I know! I'm on the trail of serendipity—of finding something I'm not looking for—whatever it is. I'll find it—but I've got to find it alone.

DERMOT: Poochie…I'm a lonely old man—I'm directing everything I have—or am—toward you. You've got many years ahead of you…I am selfish, I admit it…I want my money's worth with you…I give—you take—but I want myself to be part of the package! I'm an extra, Poochie—just like on your Mercedes—you can't have it all.

POOCHIE: Then I don't want any of it. I'll call and cancel the trip tomorrow—I'll activate the Fellowship for next term and that'll be it.

DERMOT: (*Softly*) Do you like me?

POOCHIE: Of course I like you, Uncle Dermot! You're a 'giver'…I'm not…I'm a 'taker.' You knew that—you knew that when I was a kid…when my parents cracked up, when you got my old man committed…I was all for it. I was in your own personal bleachers, waving a banner and munching a hot-dog!

DERMOT: Don't make fun of tragedy!

POOCHIE: What tragedy? He was nuts!! Mom got off scott-free…all *she* wanted was men! With all the money you settled on her, she's free to make a fool of herself for at least ten more years! She's not gonna bother her head about *me*…She could care less about the 'pooch!' (*Beat*) It's always been the two of *us*—you and me. Hell, at this point you want me but I don't want you! (*Pause*) Why should I? We haven't got one damn thing in common. Look, I've never conned you…You've always been 'Mr. Money-Bags' and I've had my hand out to accept it. (*Up*) But you don't make the rules anymore! …*I do*. And I want out of here.

DERMOT: We could have dinner once in a while. Go to the ball-game. We could sit around the club…have a drink.

POOCHIE: (*Flat*) I'm only eighteen, remember?

DERMOT: We could sit around in my study. (Beat) I wouldn't even talk. I'd just like to know what you're doing…what your next project is. (*Beat*) I wouldn't even have to talk! (*Up*) *I know I'm boring.* (*Defeated*) I just want a tiny scrap of you.

POOCHIE: (*Cold*) Should I cancel the plans for my trip?

DERMOT: No. I'll make the financial arrangements, but Mr. Carl at the bank will be the one you deal with. (*Bitter*) *You've got the money!!*

[This is one in a series of scripts Daws wrote using these characters and the characters they talk about. In some ways, it is a soap opera, but a much more realistic one than what you see on TV. These characters have a long history together and that must come through in their relationship. It should be played very intimately.]

LOVE IN VENICE
(1 Man, 1 Woman)

ENID:	He's asleep, Vincent.
VINCENT:	Don't you get tired cookin' for him?
ENID:	What cookin'? Toast and soup he has mostly. In cans. He just needs somebody to fix *whatever* he has. He's not fussy…(*Beat*) What's that look?
VINCENT:	I don't know what all this is about…we like each other. All I think about is being with you…and then when I'm with you I get this hopeless feeling, Enid.
ENID:	You want me?
VINCENT:	Don't say it like that…I get even more depressed when you say things like that…it's exciting, but…you know…
ENID:	There's nothing wrong with your wanting me. I don't like to see you sad, that's all…that's really all, Vincent.
VINCENT:	I wish it could be that simple—we'd just want each other and we'd just have each other. (*Beat*) No.
ENID:	Let's not think about it, Vincent.
VINCENT:	I don't think about it all that much…all I do think about is how peaceful I feel when I'm with you. I never had this feeling with anyone else…ever…Enid.
ENID:	I like being with you too. But we can think ahead…we can make plans… like everyone else, can't we? (*Beat*) Hmm?
VINCENT:	I don't see how. We're too young and my parents consider me a problem…and I don't have any money…and it's crazy!
ENID:	I consider my mother to be a problem.
BOTH:	CHUCKLE
VINCENT:	…but you don't see your mother. She's on the streets.

ENID:	She loves me, I guess…as much as she can love…unprofessionally, I mean. She gives me money.
VINCENT:	You think it's dirty money?
ENID:	No money is dirty…money is money. People are dirty.
VINCENT:	Let's always be friends…you're the only person I've ever been able to…what do they say, 'communicate' with? Talking to you is so…so easy…the words I use…they just seem to be right. Enid…uh…I start to say something and I look at your eyes and I know that you know what I'm gonna say. What is it, Enid…why is it like that?
ENID:	We love each other so…we're very much in love, Vincent.
VINCENT:	I don't know what love is…it's a word. My dad said something the other day about 'contentment.' Maybe that's it…I feel content when I'm with you…but only you.
ENID:	Don't get so intense about it. You like me. I like you. We're together as much as we want to be. We're not making any commitment. If you wanted me, that would be okay. For you to want me, I mean. It wouldn't solve anything. It wouldn't make the way we feel about each other any plainer. You're so intense. You want your answers right now.
VINCENT:	I went for so long a time not having any *questions*…Nothing mattered. Nothing matters all that much now…but it matters more than it did. When I think of not being with you…of your not being a part of my life, I get cold and scared.
ENID:	I'll tell you what I think…we're each other's 'answer'…The jackpot paid off for us…we'll just let the handle stay up…we won't need it anymore… we'll just scoop each other out of the cup…and walk away. Let somebody else try their luck. We've got ours…and nothing's gonna change it. You know the way I think about you, Vincent?
VINCENT:	How?
ENID:	You're the darling little puppy that won't stay off my lap.
VINCENT:	(*Chuckles*)
ENID:	That I can't chase away, even if I wanted to. That'd always come back to me, no matter what…that can't be discouraged…and you know what I am?
VINCENT:	Sure. You're my puppy.
BOTH:	<u>CHUCKLE</u>
ENID:	We don't have any defenses against each other.
VINCENT:	For the first time in my life I feel important…and I just figured out why. It's because we *are* in love. I get this proud feeling…and I

	feel conceited... like I've got something really special...that some other people think they have...but I *know* I have (*Beat*)...but when it's dark and I'm all alone...(*Pause*)
ENID:	...when it's dark and you're all alone...what?
VINCENT:	I can tell you this. It makes me feel good that I can tell you this.
ENID:	What?
VINCENT:	Sometimes I cry for you...and I'm desperate for you.
ENID:	Are you afraid I might meet somebody I'd like better than you?
VINCENT:	Oh God! It hurts so bad when you say something like that...I know it *could* happen and it's probably why I cry. (*Up*) Enid...I'm so insecure...I don't have any idea of where my life'll be going! You understand me, Enid... you do!...and I don't want to ever lose you...not have you!
ENID:	Kiss me.
VINCENT:	I love you, Enid.
ENID:	Kiss me. It's the final answer, Vincent. If my kiss doesn't tell you what our life together is going to be...there won't be any more answers...I'm frightened of your intensity and your fears...I've run out of words. Will you let my kiss tell you?
VINCENT:	Yes, Enid. (*Sigh*)
ENID:	What?
VINCENT:	It better tell me to come back tomorrow. You know what I mean, Enid? You know what I mean?

[As with all of Daws Butler's scripts, listening and reacting is a major part of the actor's job. Here, how the male character responds will differ depending on how playful the female character is played.]

TWO HAMBURGERS! — HOLD EVERYTHING!
(1 Man, 1 Woman)

WANDA: (*Calls*) Over here, Kedzey!!

KEDZEY: (*Slightly off*) O.K.

WANDA: I saved this place for you! (*Beat*) Did you get the hamburgers?

KEDZEY: Yeh, I got 'em! (*Up—annoyed*) Whatta you mean, 'you *saved* this place for *me*?'

WANDA: Whatta *you* mean, whatta *I* mean?

KEDZEY: I mean…you really complicate my life…I mean, you *saved* this 'place' for both of us, right?

WANDA: Right.

KEDZEY: Then why did you say you 'saved' it for *me*?

WANDA: I donno.

KEDZEY: Aren't *you* gonna stay here?

WANDA: Sure I'm gonna stay. You make too much out of nothing. Let's eat! I'm starved! Gimme my hamburger!

KEDZEY: At your service, madame! Here we are! Yours is the one with onions, right?

WANDA: Wrong! Mine is the one *without* onions.

KEDZEY: Without?

WANDA: Without! I can't stand onions.

KEDZEY: Question. Why did you ask for onions?

WANDA: I didn't! I said…'hold the onions…and the ketsup!'

KEDZEY: Wanda, you're mixed up.

WANDA: *I'm* mixed up?

KEDZEY: That's what I just said. Look, here it is on the paper…Here's what I wrote. (*Clears throat*) Wanda…one hamburger *with* onions! I wrote what you asked for!

WANDA: No, Kedzey…you wrote what I *didn't* ask for! I can't *stand* onions.

KEDZEY: Simmer down now…I figured it out. You take *my* hamburger and I'll take *yours*.

WANDA: O.K. (*Beat*) but there's something else.

KEDZEY: Now what?

WANDA: Does yours have mustard?

KEDZEY: No.

WANDA: No?

KEDZEY: No…I can't *stand* mustard!

WANDA: That sounds like you. (*Up*) I *love* mustard!

KEDZEY: I've got ketsup on mine. (*Beat*) Do you like ketsup?

WANDA: Don't you listen, Kedzey? I said 'hold the ketsup!'

KEDZEY: (*Up*) And I *did*! I got mustard on your hamburger!

WANDA: But you also got *onions* on my hamburger.

KEDZEY: (*Big sigh*) You're disappointed, aren't you, Wanda?

WANDA: Yes.

KEDZEY: And angry?

WANDA: Yes. I'm angry about your dumb mistake.

KEDZEY: My mistake.

WANDA: Your *dumb* mistake. You don't listen. You never listen.

KEDZEY: Sure I do. I just took it for granted that you wanted onions. Most people do. I just asked the guy for onion, automatically.

WANDA: Why didn't you ask the guy 'automatically' for onions for yourself?

KEDZEY: I forgot. I was distracted.

WANDA: Distracted? Distracted by what?

KEDZEY: There was this girl going by in this busted bikini.

WANDA: Busted?

KEDZEY: It had a rip in it…and I forgot to ask for onions myself.

WANDA: I never heard of a busted bikini before.

KEDZEY: That's why I told ya. I think you're making too much out of this whole thing, I think you should take my hamburger without the onions.

WANDA: …and the ketsup! (YUK!)

KEDZEY: …and the ketsup.

WANDA:	Yuk!
KEDZEY:	...and I'll take the one with onions and mustard.
WANDA:	We *could* do it the *other* way.
KEDZEY:	What *other* way?
WANDA:	I *could* take the hamburger with the onions and mustard.
KEDZEY:	Why?
WANDA:	Because I've been thinking, I really *despise* catsup more than I *hate* onions.
KEDZEY:	Wait a minute! Listen to this! Why don't I eat *both* hamburgers...
WANDA:	Both?
KEDZEY:	...and then I'll go and get you whatever you want. I'll listen to you this time! (*Pause*) Well, whatta you think?
WANDA:	Why should you have *two* hamburgers?
KEDZEY:	No reason...I just realized that I'd like two hamburgers. Also...it would solve the problem. And then I'll spring for two hamburgers for you—without onions *or* ketsup!
WANDA:	Never mind. You just go ahead and eat your old hamburgers. I'll get two for myself.
KEDZEY:	(*Giggles*)...and this time I'll save a place for you!
WANDA:	Never mind.
KEDZEY:	Huh?
WANDA:	I may not be back.
KEDZEY:	Boy, you *are* mad. I didn't know you were *that* mad. (*Pause*) Well, if you should get over being mad...
WANDA:	I won't.
KEDZEY:	...and decide to come back.
WANDA:	I won't. (*Pause*) But if I *do*...what?
KEDZEY:	How about bringin' me back somethin' to drink? Like a Coke.
WANDA:	(*Evil giggle*)
KEDZEY:	...or a Seven-Up...or Dr. Pepper. (*Up*) Anything but milk. I can't stand milk! Just thinkin' about that white gluckey stuff makes me gag. When I was a baby, they hadda give me ice tea. Milk! YUK!!
WANDA:	(*Sweetly*) I'd be happy to get you something to drink. I'll be right back. (*Pause*)
KEDZEY:	I *love* milk.

[*What may seem important in this scene leads to something that turns out to be trivial. The difficulty is not to give away Fred's overreaction to the audience until the end. An additional challenge is to bring to bear a sense of the past that these two characters share and allow that to color how you say the lines.*]

FRED AND TRUDY
(1 Man, 1 Woman)

FRED:	Sit in front, Trudy.
TRUDY:	I'm sitting in back, Fred.
FRED:	Aw c'mon. It's no big deal! Sit in front till we get there.
TRUDY:	No, Freddie, it doesn't make sense…we'll just have to change around…
FRED:	Trudy…
TRUDY:	(*Up*) When we pick 'em up, Dick'll sit in front with you, like he always does…and Edna'll sit in back with me!
FRED:	Dick and I talk about the Rams. You don't like me talkin' over my shoulder…
TRUDY:	You're talkin' over your shoulder now! We'll be there in ten minutes.
FRED:	Trudy, I want you in front.
TRUDY:	(*Up*) For a lousy ten minutes?
FRED:	Maybe for you, lousy…
TRUDY:	(*Firmly*) You can be so stubborn! Start the car…we're late.
FRED:	What it is, Trudy…it's what I'm used to. I like to catch you out of the corner of my eye when I'm drivin'…whether I look at you or not…
TRUDY:	Will you for God's sake, grow up, Freddie? You're hung up on patterns!
FRED:	(*Up*) That may be true, Trudy, but…it's such a simple thing I want…
TRUDY:	Fred, what you want…or think you want…is silly!
FRED:	Trudy…
TRUDY:	Fred. Listen to me. We've been over this and over this…
FRED:	I know.

TRUDY:	I'm leaving you tomorrow.
FRED:	I know that.
TRUDY:	I've…made a decision. We're going to be apart.
FRED:	I know.
TRUDY:	All my things are now at my mother's. Tonight, if you'll start this damned car, we're gonna pick up your beloved Dick and Edna and going to dinner…
FRED:	(*Down*) They're not *my* beloved Dick and Edna…
TRUDY:	Well, they're certainly not *my* beloved Dick and Edna, either! I'll be leaving them, too! Fringe benefit… and we're going to that restaurant the guy on radio talked about…
FRED:	I know that.
TRUDY:	…because we waited three months for the reservation to come through. I could care less, and probably Edna too…to me, it's an over-priced ego-trip…but you and Dick had this damn 'thing' about Basque cooking…
FRED:	I know all about that…
TRUDY:	To be brutally frank, I just want to get this night over with! I'm looking forward to the separation. (*Pause—sigh*) Mother and I will finally get around to cataloguing the pewter collection.
FRED:	(*Quietly*) How long will all this take?
TRUDY:	There's quite a bit of pewter…probably several weeks.
FRED:	…the separation…
TRUDY:	I don't know. Start the car. Pick up Dick and Edna.
FRED:	I still love you, Trudy. I don't know what I did that was so wrong. How would you like it, if, while we're separated…I decided to cat around? (*Pause*) You hear what I said, Trudy?
TRUDY:	I heard. Yes.
FRED:	How about you?
TRUDY:	I have no desire to cat around.
FRED:	You're going to catalogue pewter.
TRUDY:	(*Bitter*) I have no desire for any physical experience!
FRED:	(*Quietly*) You used to…with me. You're the only girl I ever wanted, Trudy.
TRUDY:	Start the car.
FRED:	(*Pause*) O K.
TRUDY:	Do it!
FRED:	If you change your mind, Trudy…Oh God, I hope you change your mind! I want you to sit next to me.

[This is a loving moment with the father finally coming to terms with the fact that his daughter is grown up. There should be a growing sense from him of this, as the daughter explains herself. She, in turn must alternate between gently confronting him and teasing him.]

FATHER AND DAUGHTER
(1 Man, 1 Woman)

SUSAN:	(*Surprised*) Dad! You still up? It's four-thirty!
DAD:	Still up…yeh.
SUSAN:	(*Light laugh*) But why? (*As Shirley Temple*) Gee, Colonel! I'm a *big* girl now! *I'm* not a-scared of those ole *Yankees!*
DAD:	I dozed off in the chair…woke up…looked at the clock. Looked in your room…
SUSAN:	Oh Dad! Come off it! You knew I was with Ben! (*Excited*)…and Dad, listen! Ben's Uncle Chad has this old trailer he was gonna get rid of. Junk, he said. He asked Ben if he could use it…have to be fixed up and everything, but Ben could have it if he wants! Isn't that wonderful!!
DAD:	You lost me somewhere.
SUSAN:	Dad, it's the answer to all our prayers! With that old piece of junk, we can start out to build his church…
DAD:	Huh?
SUSAN:	Ben's got his degree in Sociology and somewhere out there…in the boondocks or wherever—he means to reach people…to help people! Dad, he's got so much to give…(*Up*) and now we've got wheels!!
DAD:	Susan…what'd you say about you and Ben?
SUSAN:	I said we're going away together…in the junky old trailer!
DAD:	Just like that?
SUSAN:	(*Levels*) Get that look off your face, Dad…this should come as no great surprise…you knew the way Ben and I felt about each other. (*Pause—emphasize*) Dad! I am over twenty-one!
DAD:	You better go to bed now…we'll talk about it later.

SUSAN:	(*Annoyed—hurt*) Talk about it! I love Ben and that's it!
DAD:	Forgive me, Susan…I was coming on a little strong. I'm fond of Ben, you know that…
SUSAN:	Somewhere along the line, we'll get married…
DAD:	(*Suddenly*) Susan, what it is…I don't wanna let go. I can't accept the idea of your going. I'll miss you so!
SUSAN:	I'll miss you too, Dad.
DAD:	When are you going? You and Ben?
SUSAN:	Soon. Oh, blessed word…'soon!'…we've been waiting so long. Ben'll be building his church at last!
DAD:	…and what will you be doing?
SUSAN:	I'll be working…waitress, clerk…it doesn't matter. I'll support us as long as I have too. (*Change—warm*) Dad, you've gotta realize something…Ben isn't just a 'man' to me…he's a hope for a decent life…and I do love him as a man. There's a strength he has. Dad…he believes in himself. He believes in what he can do for others.
DAD:	How long's it been since you first met Ben?
SUSAN:	Six months…about that. Could be forever!
DAD:	(*Quickly*) You've been lovers?
SUSAN:	Do you really want me to tell you, Dad?
DAD:	…Susan…
SUSAN:	(*Quietly*) Were you and Mom lovers? Before, I mean?
DAD:	Forgive me, Susan.
SUSAN:	I said that Ben is more than a man to me…but he is a man. I love him.
DAD:	(*Change*) Susan…over the years, you've been slipping away from me…
SUSAN:	I've grown up, Dad.
DAD:	I miss my little girl. (*Softly*) I cherish you, Susan.
SUSAN:	I know.
DAD:	You're all I have left.
SUSAN:	(*Softly*) No, Daddy—that's not true. You have yourself.
DAD:	Myself?
SUSAN:	You're a person. There's life around you.
DAD:	When your mother died, I felt an emptiness…but an emptiness of dimension. Outside of it, there was you. I felt profound grief…not at mother's going…but, because {I've never told you this,

	Susan)…because in all of our years together, she'd never been completely mine!
SUSAN:	(*Sympathy*) Oh, Daddy!
DAD:	She was a…private person, Susan. She wanted to, I think, but she never let me know who she 'was'…
	(*Softly*) but I loved her…and that was enough (*Sigh*) and when the pain came…at the end…I cried out to God for her release!
SUSAN:	Daddy…Daddy…
DAD:	Her presence has never left this house.
SUSAN:	I know. Sometimes, I close my eyes and she's here… with me. I think of her all the time…(*Change*) I remember, when I was little…I remember when she'd touch me, I'd turn my head like a kitten…so she wouldn't take her hand away.
DAD:	We loved you so.
SUSAN:	You and Mom were always there. I accepted your caring, your generosity…
DAD:	…and love?
SUSAN:	…mostly your love. It was my security. I remember, behind all the little islands of happiness I knew… that I was also very frightened.
DAD:	(*Softly*) We all are, Susan…usually of ourselves. (*Change*) To me, Susan, you've always been a little girl…a wide-eyed…trusting…child. (*Almost to himself*) Even now, when I look in a window and I see a toy you would have liked I want to get it for you. Oh, Susan…to know one more time, your delight—how you used to jump up and down and say 'I love it! I love it!' You never saved the ribbon…you just tore off the paper…you couldn't wait!…and then I'd feel your arms around me!
SUSAN:	But Daddy…you do buy me toys! I find those toys in the old 'secret places.'
DAD:	You found the toys?
SUSAN:	(*Scolds*) Daddy! You know I did! It's the little game we play…those little extra hugs I gave you. You knew why.
DAD:	Are you still frightened, Susan?
SUSAN:	A little…but with Ben…since Ben…I've felt a peace, a strength…it's our strength, Ben's and mine.
DAD:	(*Change*) It's late, Susan… (*Softly*) little girl. (*Smiles*) You've gotta get started on some trailer curtains tomorrow!
SUSAN:	(*Laughs lightly*) Today, Daddy…today!!

[Couples act differently depending on how long they've been together. This couple has been together for a long time and there should be a level of familiarity and comfort to their conversation.]

HOME IS WHERE THE HEART IS
(1 Man, 1 Woman)

BERNIE:	Look, Brenda, if we're not going—let's accept it…there's a couple things I'd like to watch on TV.
BRENDA:	I wanted to go…I know you didn't give a damn whether we did or not.
BERNIE:	Whatta you mean? I wanted to go…but just not very much.
BRENDA:	You didn't want to go at all. When I first mentioned the party three weeks ago, you groaned.
BERNIE:	I *always* groan when you mention a party. (*Beat*) I don't like parties.
BRENDA:	I do.
BERNIE:	Then *you* go. I have always thought the great American Party a bore!
BRENDA:	Oh God!
BERNIE:	I'm an iconoclast of sorts…
BRENDA:	'Out of sorts!'
BERNIE:	That too…I don't dig the traditional—the so-called 'party'…it's not a party…it's a bunch of dull couples sharing their dullness with others, instead of each other.
BRENDA:	Some people have 'fun!'
BERNIE:	They 'they' should *go*! *I* don't have fun—I am bored out of my skull! {*Up*} *You* on the other hand, *aren't* bored out of your skull…so why don't you…*go*, for God's sake!! Have Arthur and Louella pick you up and you go with *them*, for Christ's sake!!
BRENDA:	Why are you always 'putting down' Arthur and Louella? You think you're so much better than them?
BERNIE:	Arthur is a jerk. Louella defies classification.
BRENDA:	He's a 'college graduate!'…She's working on her thesis!

BERNIE:	…and he has a fifty-footer in the Marina that can sleep seven. That always got me—why seven? Who does he take, three swinging couples…and a priest?
BRENDA:	Shut up!
BERNIE:	I thought that was kinda clever.
BRENDA:	Shut up!
BERNIE:	Instant replay from my wife! (*Change*) Look, Brenda…I am so fed up playing along with the syndrome…and now, I've just had it!! I've had it, right!!
BRENDA:	If you'd called the garage an hour ago—before they went home, they might have brought over a 'loaner' …we could have gone to the party! At the last minute, you tell me the car's dead…when did you know it was dead?
BERNIE:	*At the last minute*! While you were getting dressed, I went out to see if the heater was working all right…and it wouldn't turn over…the engine, I mean.
BRENDA:	You should have joined the automobile club! (*Change*) Checking the heater…on a night like tonight! My God!
BERNIE:	It's chilly…the house is a barn, if you want the truth!
BRENDA:	Chilly!! I'm burning up!!
BERNIE:	To me…chilly…yeh!
BRENDA:	*Put on a sweater if you're chilly*…we're trying to save energy. You never know what the hell's going on!!
BERNIE:	I know what the hell *I* want to be going on! Am I my world's keeper?
BRENDA:	Doris wasn't too happy about our not coming.
BERNIE:	Doris? Listen, if Doris was gonna spit and there was the gutter and me…where d'ya think Doris'd spit?
BRENDA:	I don't like to be asked 'baby questions.'
BERNIE:	Why was Doris upset?
BRENDA:	That statue-maker from Cleveland was gonna be at the party…the one she wanted you to meet…she thought maybe you could use him in the model department.
BERNIE:	Why do you call him a statue-maker…he's a sculptor.
BRENDA:	What difference does it make—you know what I mean!
BERNIE:	So…actually, that's why Doris wanted me at the party—so I could meet her sculptor?
BRENDA:	Contacts *are* made at parties, sometimes.
BERNIE:	Well, we're not going—we can't go, for God's sake!! We don't have

	any transportation!! So I'm gonna watch Barney Miller and have a beer…and enjoy myself.
BRENDA:	…and just forget about a party that's been planned for several weeks now.
BERNIE:	Nothing I can do about it.
BRENDA:	Arthur and Louella could have picked us up.
BERNIE:	Have them pick *you* up…if you wanna go to the party so bad. (*Change*) Get on the phone, call 'em…tell 'em you'd like to go.
BRENDA:	How about you?
BERNIE:	I *don't* wanna go.
BRENDA:	They'll wonder why you're not going.
BERNIE:	Just tell them I wanna enjoy myself watching Barney Miller and drinking a bottle of beer. Simple pleasure for simple me!
BRENDA:	You're hopeless!
BERNIE:	At least it's definite! I'm hopeless—no where else to go! I'm hopeless! Call Arthur and Louella!
BRENDA:	What about the Waltons?
BERNIE:	You want them to pick you up?
BRENDA:	You are so funny! I might like to watch 'The Waltons'…aren't they on when Barney Miller is?
BERNIE:	They're pre-empted—Christmas special—bye-bye, Waltons! Some schlocky cartoon dreck is taking over tonight!!
BRENDA:	Why doesn't some schlocky cartoon dreck ever take over the Barney Miller show?
BERNIE:	Because…while there isn't much…there is *some* justice in the world! (*Change*) You gonna stay home with me—and have a beer and watch Barney Miller?
BRENDA:	I don't know about the beer…and I don't know about Barney Miller. I may read.
BERNIE:	Suit yourself. It's a big house. A lotta rooms. We can have together-ness even if we have to yell!!
BRENDA:	I know one thing…it's too damn hot in here!!
BERNIE:	Well, don't for god's sake, open a window!…*take off a sweater*!

[Some of Daws' scripts play more like an inter view with one character getting new information out of the other. This can make for some nice tension and "give and take" between characters. Daws liked the actor to orchestrated the script beforehand. But he also expected the actor to concentrate on listening to the other character and reacting naturally rather than on how to say your lines.]

THIEVES AMONG US
(2 Women)

ARLENE:	Good to see you, Teddy! I had 'em fix the shades so we could sit by the window…you always like to sit by the window. Gerald's our waiter—good old Gerald!
TEDDY:	But with the shades fixed, we can't see anything.
ARLENE:	The sun's gonna move—Gerald can open 'em in ten minutes or so—and then you'll have your view.
TEDDY:	The view isn't all that important. Not anymore, I mean.
ARLENE:	For romantics, a view is always important. (*Change*) You wanna drink? I'm having a rum Tom Collins—touch of nutmeg, a drop of pistachio extract…Eddie gets it somewhere.
TEDDY:	Good?
ARLENE:	It's ok.
TEDDY:	(*Giggle*) You never change. You used to do this in school…come up with some idea as if it's the most super idea in the whole world—and then when we'd sort of enthuse about it—you'd shrug it off as something ordinary.
ARLENE:	Nobody changes. Not really—we just wear bigger sizes.
TEDDY:	How long's Eddie been tending bar?
ARLENE:	Eddie was born here, I think…I think the bar rag used to be his diaper. (*Giggle*) Let's ask him!
TEDDY:	(*Giggle*) He's been here a long time, I know that. I came here for my first 'drinking' date—he was a bartender *then*.
ARLENE:	Do you remember?
TEDDY:	What I had to drink? Eddie probably would!!
ARLENE:	No, dummy! Who your *date* was! I remember, if you don't.
TEDDY:	(*Serious*) It was Bud. First the malt-shops…and then this.

ARLENE:	That was…how many years ago?
TEDDY:	Four…five…and a few months.
ARLENE:	Bud stops by the office sometimes. He looks good.
TEDDY:	He stops by your office?
ARLENE:	He plays golf with Mr. Thompson once in a while—they were involved in some deal…He swipes paper clips.
TEDDY:	Bud does? Paper clips?
ARLENE:	He's a petty crook, didn't you know that? He's wanted in several offices around town. I remember when we were in school, he used to steal the kids' lunch money. Go through pockets in the cloak room.
TEDDY:	How'd you know?
ARLENE:	He stole mine one day…I caught him at it. I was gonna turn him in.
TEDDY:	Did you?
ARLENE:	No.
TEDDY:	How come?
ARLENE:	You know what he did? He took my face in his hands and kissed me right on the lips…I'd never been kissed like that before…and this was the fifth grade! He said he was sorry—he said he liked me—he wouldn't steal *my* money.
TEDDY:	But he did.
ARLENE:	He said it was a mistake. (*Change*) Anyway, I never turned him in. (*Change*) He's made up for it a few times.
TEDDY:	Whatta you mean?
ARLENE:	He's taken me to lunch a few times since then.
TEDDY:	He never told me about it.
ARLENE:	You were going with him. Why make waves?
TEDDY:	But why didn't he tell me—I wouldn't have minded.
ARLENE:	Bud can't do things right out in the open…he likes to sidle around buildings with his back to the wall.
TEDDY:	We haven't been seeing each other much lately.
ARLENE:	You break up?
TEDDY:	Just circumstances. He's had to go out of town a lot recently.
ARLENE:	He never mentioned it to me.
TEDDY:	Why would he mention it to you?
ARLENE:	I told you he stops off at the office once in a while…we get to talking—couple times there, he took me to lunch—he's always

conveniently without any money or his credit card—but it doesn't matter…he's an original and he's fun to be with. Last week, we got to talking…and had a few drinks and I got hell from Mr. Thompson for being so late!

TEDDY: (*Quietly*) How late were you?

ARLENE: I was supposed to be back at one fifteen…Bud got me back at three-thirty! He probably has those long lunches with you, right?

TEDDY: I told you I hadn't seen much of Bud lately…he's broken several dates—went out of town—promised to call…didn't. When's the last time *you* had lunch with him?

ARLENE: Day before yesterday.

TEDDY: In Cleveland?

ARLENE: What?

TEDDY: That's where he *was*.

ARLENE: In Cleveland? He told you he was in Cleveland?

TEDDY: He cancelled a weekend in Santa Barbara we'd planned on for a long time…quick call to Cleveland. (*Change*) You sure you got back to work at three-thirty?

ARLENE: What're you saying?

TEDDY: I'm saying I had to do a lot of fast talking to get off early on Friday for that weekend that never was…and now you tell me he was in *town*! (*Change*) Why didn't he spend the *rest* of the day with you?

ARLENE: If you want the truth, Bud told me he had to get me back because he had a heavy date.

TEDDY: He tell you with who? (*Pause*) Did you assume it was me?

ARLENE: I didn't give it that much thought.

TEDDY: You knew I was going with him…and you call *him* a thief!

ARLENE: We didn't talk about you. We talked about his new video recorder. He'd just got it. He was very enthused about it.

TEDDY: *What* video recorder?

ARLENE: His new one—I told you he was a petty crook—it was 'hot'—he got it for two hundred…some junky needed cash.

TEDDY: (*Slowly*) Oh God!

ARLENE: He asked, did I want to see it—so we went up to his place…don't know how he can afford it…the place, I mean.

TEDDY: …and you saw it.

ARLENE: I saw it.

TEDDY: Was it nice?

ARLENE:	Whatta you mean, was it 'nice?' The video recorder?
TEDDY:	It took quite a while to really see it…right? I mean, properly.
ARLENE:	It was brand-new. He was telling me what it could do.
TEDDY:	He always liked things that were brand-new. Did he tell you the things *he* could do?
ARLENE:	(*Abruptly*) Let's go! I don't like where this is going.
TEDDY:	Might as well…I was waving Gerald away with my eyes.
ARLENE:	Bud takes what he wants, for Christ's sake! He stuck with you longer than anybody!
TEDDY:	Off and on.
ARLENE:	Oh shut up!…I don't know what the hell's the point, my going gentle into what was my good night…Bud got me back at three-thirty the *next day*! (*Goes on*) I'd seen him *before* too! If the police put out WANTED posters on Bud—they wouldn't be in the Post Office!—d'ya know where they'd be?—In every Lady's Room in town!! Wake up, kid! You were going with a thief—he stole you blind—he got everything out of you he wanted—he tried it with me—I didn't have the holding power you did! If he ever loved anybody…it was you! It was you, Teddy!
TEDDY:	None of this surprises me too much. I knew he was a thief. I caught him stealing my father's typewriter—one weekend they went to the beach and I stayed home.
ARLENE:	You caught him?
TEDDY:	Putting it in his trunk.
ARLENE:	You didn't turn him in? You didn't tell your father?
TEDDY:	I made him put it back. He knew I was gonna turn him in.
ARLENE:	And…
TEDDY:	He didn't take my sweet little sixteen-year-old face in his hands and *kiss me*. (*Pause—sigh*) We went up to my room and he…he…
ARLENE:	(*Slyly*)…talked you out of it?…or *into* it?
TEDDY:	*Something* like that…I'd never known anybody like him. I figured better me than the typewriter. I really loved him.
ARLENE:	(*Brightly*) Let's have lunch! The hell with him!!…O.K.?
TEDDY:	Why not?…but not here…Gerald can leave the shades alone—I'll find me another view.

[This dialogue features something Daws liked to play with often: characters who try to prove they are smarter than the other. There is competitive streak in both of them and even though they are talking of trivial matters, they are having a battle of words.]

WORDS GET BANDIED ABOUT
(1 Man, 1 Woman)

CLAUDE:	I want a believable explanation. You got out of line and I want to know why. That's all.
MAUDE:	I gave you an explanation.
CLAUDE:	…but *not* a 'believable' one.
MAUDE:	I believed it.
CLAUDE:	…and so did your mother.
MAUDE:	She had it notarized. I mean, she should have.
CLAUDE:	(*Up*) Don't give me your smart remarks! You're becoming impossible, Maude! Where is the little girl who took my hand and looked up at me with such innocent trust? The little girl who listened to my stories?
MAUDE:	You don't believe *me*…I didn't believe your *untrue stories*.
CLAUDE:	Stories don't have to be true! Why can't you understand that? Stories are just that…'stories!'…
MAUDE:	They're words that somebody made up.
CLAUDE:	Does that make them any less real?
MAUDE:	The words didn't just 'happen.'
CLAUDE:	But they 'could have!'…that's the point I'm trying to make! (*Change of thought*) Do you ever read the newspaper?
MAUDE:	I *listen* to the news on TV. It's just news…it's not a story. I *look* at the news too.
CLAUDE:	Do you believe what you *hear*?…and what you *see*?
MAUDE:	Sometimes. (*Pause*) I guess I believe it all, but…
CLAUDE:	- but 'what?'
MAUDE:	…but I don't *like* to believe it. Some of it makes me feel bad. And

there's nothing I can do to help. Sometimes I'm sorry I watch or listen to the news at all!!

CLAUDE: But you do watch it. Everybody does. They feel that it's some sort of 'duty'—that it's an obligation they owe to the television station for all the trouble they've taken.

MAUDE: Trouble?

CLAUDE: All the time they've spent gathering it.

MAUDE: Like a farmer.

CLAUDE: What?

MAUDE: Like a farmer. He plants seeds. They grow. Then he cuts them down. Then he sells them to markets.

CLAUDE: Yeh. That's the idea. What if the farmer grew all this stuff and nobody bought it.

MAUDE: You mean…what if it just laid there on the ground…

CLAUDE: Or in a tree.

MAUDE: …and nobody made it into food.

CLAUDE: The farmer would have to declare bankruptcy. He'd have to sell all his farm tools; his tractors and his reaper; and he'd have to fire all of his helpers.

MAUDE: …and then they'd become a burden to the State.

CLAUDE: They'd have to go to the unemployment office and take whatever job was offered them.

MAUDE: Maybe they'd get a 'better' job. Being a worker on a farm can't be all that much fun.

CLAUDE: It's not supposed to be 'fun.' Work is work. You work because you have to take care of yourself…

MAUDE: …and your family…if you've got a family.

CLAUDE: Right!

MAUDE: Work is fun for some people. What about a movie star?

CLAUDE: They have to work hard.

MAUDE: But they get a lot of money. It's fun.

CLAUDE: It's not all that much 'fun.' Unless you're the star of the picture…you're sort of pushed around…and even ignored. You're just another prop.

MAUDE: What's a 'prop?'

CLAUDE: You know what a prop is!

MAUDE: Do I?

CLAUDE: I thought you did.

MAUDE:	What does it mean?
CLAUDE:	Actually, it's short for 'property.'
MAUDE:	Like 'real-estate?'
CLAUDE:	It could, but it doesn't mean that in the theatre.
MAUDE:	...or the movie studio.
CLAUDE:	Sometimes it's a chair. Or a cigar. Or a telephone. It's something the actor uses when he's performing.
MAUDE:	Women don't use 'em?
CLAUDE:	I was including 'women' when I said 'he's'...
MAUDE:	Why didn't you say 'when he or she is performing?'
CLAUDE:	I didn't think it was necessary. I thought our under-standing of each other would supply the inference.
MAUDE:	What's a...
CLAUDE:	(*Quickly*) An *inference* is a reference to something or somebody who exists in a secondary way. To something or somebody who is not excluded but whose presence is assumed.
MAUDE:	Why should a woman be an inference?
CLAUDE:	She *shouldn't* be. The listener should just assume that she's included.
MAUDE:	I didn't.
CLAUDE:	You wouldn't.
MAUDE:	What does that mean?
CLAUDE:	It means that you seem to go out of your way to mix me up. You keep me constantly on edge. The words I must select in our discussions are like eggs that I mustn't crush.
MAUDE:	I thought you said we didn't have discussions.
CLAUDE:	I inferred that, in a way. But what I really said was 'what happened to the little girl who listened to my stories?'
MAUDE:	Nothing happened to her. She's just decided she wants to say it and tell it like it is.
CLAUDE:	Like Howard Cosell?
MAUDE:	If you want.
CLAUDE:	I wish you weren't turning off on stories. Stories can be more interest-ing than reality...and they can be controlled. (*Pause*) Reality can't.
MAUDE:	Truth is trouble.
CLAUDE:	I think so. Truth is trouble.
MAUDE:	Tell me a story.

[This could easily be played as a comic flight of fancy. The challenge is to make it seem real.]

ITALIAN CAFE SCENE
(1 Man, 1 Woman)

PERSON: I found this little restaurant the other night—Never heard of the place. Antonio's. It was set back from the street—very unpretentious. I dropped in about eight-thirty, Saturday night.

SOUND: DOOR OPEN—BELL TINKLE

There was no bar. No wine cellar that I could see. Just a Coke machine in the corner, (*Beat*) it was out-of-order.

CHEF: (*Comes on*) Come in! Come in! So nice to see you!

PERSON: You must be Antonio.

CHEF: Hey, you pretty smart. You figure that out!

PERSON: I'm quick.

CHEF: I gotta 'pologize cuz I got no waitress here. I'm no busy an' I tell her take the night off.

PERSON: But this is Saturday night—you're not busy on Saturday night?

CHEF: Well, I'm busier now than mos' time.

PERSON: How many customers you got tonight?

CHEF: One.

PERSON: One?

CHEF: You. Siddown. Whatta you gonna have?

PERSON: I haven't seen the menu.

CHEF: You wanna know somethin'? I ain't seen it myself. It's around here someplace — where I put that menu?

PERSON: You only got one?

CHEF: When I need more I'll get more.

PERSON: It doesn't matter—just bring me the specialty of the house.

CHEF: I got no specialty—everything is special. You tell me what you want—I make it for you.

PERSON: How about my favorite—chicken Cacciatore?

CHEF: I dunno how to make that.

PERSON: Veal Scaloppini?

CHEF: I dunno how to make that.

PERSON: How about Scampi? Lasagna? Eggplant Parmesan?

CHEF: I dunno…

PERSON: How about good ole spaghetti and meatballs? (*Up*) I know, you don't know how…

CHEF: (*Up*) *I know how*!

PERSON: Good.

CHEF: I know how to make it—but you wouldn't like it.

PERSON: How do you know?

CHEF: Why you so different from everybody else?

PERSON: Antonio, I don't get it—you don't have a wine cellar, you don't have a bar. No waitress. You can't cook and you don't have any customers…

CHEF: I know—sometimes I wish I didn't love the restaurant business so much!!!

[Another scene from one of Daws' Sherlock Holmes radio plays. One of the challenges here is to make Dr. Watson a believable real person and not a bumbling cartoon character like he was in the movies. There are many ways to play Glynnis (chatty, hesitant, hiding something, cooperative, manipulative, or other possibilities).]

GLYNNIS (British)
(1 Man, 1 Woman)

GLYNNIS: (*Weak—embarrassed*) I'm so sorry I fainted. Doctor.

WATSON: (*Concerned*) You feel better now.

GLYNNIS: Much better. Thank dear Mrs. Hudson for the soup. It was delicious.

WATSON: I will. I will, Glynnis.

GLYNNIS: (*A bit stronger*) I must go now. I've troubled you enough. You'll talk to Mr. Holmes…and perhaps he can help me as he has helped others.

WATSON: About Clifford. (*Up*) Oh, Glynnis, I wish you had come here immediately. My heart aches to see how you have been torturing yourself with worry—not eating.

GLYNNIS: I thought he'd come back…that he would let me know if he was all right.

WATSON: He left because of the argument?

GLYNNIS: It was a fight, Doctor Watson—I threw things at him. (*Slight sob*) I'm so ashamed now. Oh God! If only I knew he was all right! If he doesn't want me anymore…I can accept that—but I don't want him to be hurt.

WATSON: Holmes will get to the bottom of it. (*Change*) Don't you have any idea of where he might have gone…to cool off, let us say?

GLYNNIS: It might be Jane.

WATSON: Jane?

GLYNNIS: She's written him several times. He would wait for the postman…but one day the postman was late and I saw a letter. He confessed to others. Said they meant nothing…but I don't know.

WATSON: Who is Jane?

GLYNNIS:	A dancer. They were to be married and she jilted him. It was a traumatic experience for him…he was very shy, not at ease with women. He loved her quickly and deeply…attended her every performance. He met her, finally, through a mutual friend. It was the romance of his life. (*Softly*) He never spoke of it to me…but a woman knows.
WATSON:	How did you two meet?
GLYNNIS:	His sister…Kitty…introduced us. The three of us went to concerts—picnics. He…liked me.
WATSON:	When did he profess his love for you?
GLYNNIS:	Not too long afterward. It flattered me. I had always been in love with him and yet, down deep, I knew…I really knew that I would be only a substitute. (*Sobs*) Oh. Doctor Watson!…I want him back! Even if he doesn't want me…I want Clifford to be all right!

[This is the third in a series of scripts Daws wrote about mediocre English poet, Edgerton Voss who is visiting America, and his adoring fan, Manta Ray (married to Herbie Ray). Try not to take every line at face value. Perhaps Manta has some feelings for Edgerton she is not expressing.]

EDGERTON VOSS STEPS OUT – BUT NOT TOO FAR
(Man—British and Woman—American)

SOUND:	PHONE RINGS ONCE – PICK UP
MANTA:	Hello? This is Manta. You expected it to be Manta, didn't you? (*Beat*)

Well, then! I *always* recognize your voice… You're the only Englishman I know. (Up) Why do I…what? Well, why not? I mean, I pick up the phone on the first ring if I'm by the phone, because…well, why not? What'd you ask me a dumb question like that for? I don't think there's anything psychological about letting it ring four or five times … you think I want people to think I'm too busy to answer on the first ring? I'm not that insecure … I save my play-acting for when I'm in bed! (*Giggles*) I said that because I know you like it when I put Herbie's masculinity down. (*Beat*) Oh come on now, you know you lust after me! If I'd underwrite it, you'd run away with me in minute! (*Giggle*) Maybe I'll let the phone ring when you call – just let it ring and ring – let it ring off the hook – I just won't answer it at all – then you'll really think I'm busy. My not answering the phone will be your busy signal. (*Goes on*) Y'know, I really should be busy when you call – it's always some new gimmick to 'use' me … or embarrass me. You want a 'call-back' to my Great Books Meeting … so you can read some dirty haikus or something? (*Giggle*) It's not that bad an idea. The ladies loved the other dirty poetry you read – the Bawdy Ballads. Loved 'em! You'd be surprised at how many wanted copies! Each one thought she was the only one asking. You were a smash, Edgie! (*Change*) I'll be home for a while … I'm going out to mulch the marijuana later on … but I'll be here for an hour or so. (*Beat*) O.K. come on by. (*Up*) Why can't you tell me what you want on the phone? O.K.… I'll put another pot of coffee on and I've got

	three of my almond croissants left … you can have two! One more thing … Herbie marked the brandy level … so watch it!! Bye, Sneaky Pete!
SOUND:	PHONE HANGS UP
(*Pause*)	
SOUND:	KNOCK ON DOOR
MANTA:	It's open! Come on in!
SOUND:	DOOR OPEN – CLOSE
VOSS:	*That* wasn't very bright!
MANTA:	What wasn't, Mr. Bones?
VOSS:	Just saying 'come on in!' like that … what if it hadn't been me? What if it'd been some blackguard?
MANTA:	I wouldn't have said 'Come in!' (*Beat*) Think about it.
VOSS:	If I'd thought about it, I might have come to that same conclusion myself … is that what you're trying to tell me.
MANTA:	It *is* what I *am* telling you.
VOSS:	Where're the almond croissants?
MANTA:	It's on the table.
VOSS:	'It's' … on the table?
MANTA:	Huh?
VOSS:	'It's' … on the table?
MANTA:	It's what we use for eating – a table. It works out.
VOSS:	You said I'd have 'two' croissants!
MANTA:	You're right, I did. I gave you two – I was just teasing.
VOSS:	(*Pause*) You didn't warm them up?
MANTA:	I just made 'em this morning… for Herbie's breakfast.
VOSS:	I assume that Herbie's were warm.
MANTA:	Right out of the oven.
VOSS:	One would be led to believe that you are more considerate of Herbie's desires than mine.
MANTA:	Herbie beats me if I don't give him hot croissants.
VOSS:	Especially if he's had a cold roll in the hay … as they say.
MANTA:	(*Giggle*) Oh you!! Here, I'll heat 'em up – just take a second in the ole microwave. I was gonna do it anyway … I just can't resist playing this little game we always play.
VOSS:	… and at which you always lose.
MANTA:	(*Giggle*) What'd you have to tell me that was so important?

VOSS:	Simply this. I met someone who has set me back on my heels, goody, goody! It's a line from an old American song, but it's pertinent to my present situation. (*Beat*) She's a waitress at a British Hash-house. Food tastes like homemade ... ample but awful – the wine list is a pamphlet. I go there occasionally, at the bequest of a few of my penny-pinching English cronies. I keep the conversation alive – and for which consideration I am given to eat and drink with them. I am not limited in any way. I may order anything on the menu ... although the special entrees on the Early-Bird Special are not too subtly brought to my attention. (*Quickly*) Dismissed, of course!
MANTA:	...because you stick to the 'Big Menu.'
VOSS:	Like epoxy! It's just as inedible but plentiful!!
MANTA:	...and where does this waitress come in?
VOSS:	She became aware of me...the second or third time I was there... she seemed fascinated by what my stomach could endure – but beyond that what seemed to be my overt...verbosity.
MANTA:	...and what is it really?
VOSS:	...my overt verbosity. I don't want it to go any further than this room...but I *am* verbose. Sometimes witty ... sometimes brilliant but verbosity is the 'meat'n'potatos' of my disregarded compendium. I do not abbreviate or summarize.
MANTA:	It's an endearing annoyance.
VOSS:	Maybelle listened to my expository gems on several occasions... her silvery laughter joining that of the others! It warmed me! I found myself, once again, the small boy showing off for the approval of a girl he found attractive.
MANTA:	...and she spoke to you?
VOSS:	(*Quietly*) Yes.
MANTA:	What'd she say?
VOSS:	She said – now I'm not going to try and imitate her voice or even approximate the definitive reading of her line –
MANTA:	(*Giggle*) Oh you!! Get on with it!!
VOSS:	She said – you're the only one in your party who didn't order the Early-Bird special.
MANTA:	Put *that* in your memory-book for sure!
VOSS:	I asked her when she got off duty.
MANTA:	...and she told you?
VOSS:	...and she told me. Then I asked her if she had a car.

MANTA:	You're something!
VOSS:	Well, let's face it! All of my 'rides' would've been gone – and I'd have no way of returning to my digs.
MANTA:	Did she have a car?
VOSS:	A darling little Toyota!! I must remember to get it back to her. (*Continues*) At any rate, or any other 'trash phrase' which would act as an on-ramp to the freeway of my continuity ... we have been seeing each other. From the first, I was quite outspoken with her. I said 'Your place or the YMCA?'
MANTA:	(*Giggles*) Are you smitten with ... (*Up*) What's her name?
VOSS:	Maybelle. She doesn't hyphenate it, but when I say it out loud or think it, I add a hyphen of my own ... May-belle cries out for a hyphen!
MANTA:	Are...you smitten with Maybelle?
VOSS:	To the point of distraction. She is on my mind constantly. Ways to please her – being aware of the responsibility of my love. I must get her car back to her.
MANTA:	She loaned you her car?
VOSS:	Yes.
MANTA:	But you don't have a driver's license yet.
VOSS:	I don't have a dentist either...but my teeth can still hurt.
MANTA:	Hard logic to fight.
VOSS:	I'm being most careful of it. I wheeled up to Big Bear over the weekend ... I never had a way of getting there before.
MANTA:	Alone?
VOSS:	...and lonely too, I might add.
MANTA:	You didn't take hyphenated Maybelle with you?
VOSS:	Manta, think of what you're saying! Maybelle is, after all, a maiden lady!
MANTA:	You could have got two cabins.
VOSS:	I have no intention of wasting her money that way. I feel guilty enough using her Texaco Credit card for gas.
MANTA:	You're going just a little too fast for me.
VOSS:	I'm going much too fast for you, my darling Manta.
MANTA:	I think you're making all of this up. I feel like such a gooney, falling right in your trap!
VOSS:	The lady exists. May-belle 'is' ... my heart is no longer my own.
MANTA:	...and what do you want from me?

VOSS:	Your advice. Just that…we have similar affinities. Intellectually, we are compatable. The little heart goes pitty-pat when I look into her eyes – and my ego permits me to accept a like palpitation emanating from her aorta area.
MANTA:	You do have a way of nut-shelling things.
VOSS:	Don't be unkind! We're 'gone' on each other, kid! I think she wants me to move in with her – with all that implies.
MANTA:	You mean her carrying your trunk upstairs?
VOSS:	Again…I implore you not to be unkind! I'm quite serious about this….the love experience is one I have never known, and I look to you for guidance.
MANTA:	Whatever.
VOSS:	If she should ask me to marry her…what should I do? Would you and Herbie give me away?
MANTA:	We wouldn't tell her anything nasty…is that what you mean?
VOSS:	(*Chuckles*) What I really mean, dear Manta … is that I do think – quite seriously – that I have come upon a remarkable woman. I am flattered that she likes me. She humbles me. I want you and Herbie to meet her. (*Up*) After all, Manta … you two are the only family I have over here!
MANTA:	Of course we will, Edgie. Now I've only got one question for you.
VOSS:	Ask away!
MANTA:	Where'll it be – our place… or hers? (*They chuckle together*)

[This piece is about what happened during dinner not what is happening during the scene. Much of the history is in the script for you to find and use as emotional weight to what your character is saying.]

DISHWASHER 'HANDS'
(2 Men, 1 Woman)

BARNEY:	(*Calls*) Jane! (*Beat*) Hey, Jane! We got any clean glasses?
JANE:	(*Off*) In the dishwasher, Barney!
BARNEY:	(*Calls*) Clean?
JANE:	(*Off*) Not yet.
BARNEY:	(*Calls*) Well...*when*?
JANE:	(*Off*) When they're washed.
BARNEY:	(*Calls*) And when'll that be, Jane?
JANE:	(*Off*) When the dishwasher is filled up and turned on. I'll prob'ly start it after supper.
BARNEY:	(*Normal*) Never mind.
JANE:	(*Calls*) You mad? You sound mad, Barney.
BARNEY:	(*Calls*) I'm frustrated! Every time I want a glass, a cup, a dish, a spoon...they're always in the damn dishwasher!
JANE:	(*Calls*) You bought it for me.
BARNEY:	Forget it. Don't worry about it!
JANE:	(*Off*) I'm not worried. Somehow, the dishes always get washed.
BARNEY:	(*To someone*) What the hell, Tod...whatta we need glasses for anyway. We'll just drink '*em outta* the can!
TOD:	Sound reasoning! I wouldn't have eavesdropped but I forget my earplugs. Domestic unrest upsets me. (*Up*) Beer tastes better from the can anyway...it's the only way.
BARNEY:	What Jane and I had was sort of a 'tiff.'
TOD:	That's the way I accepted it—there were no big guns—no forced marches—no screaming headlines.

BARNEY:	Jane and I get along fine in the important essentials—but this dishwasher drives me nuts! I don't let Jane know it, but half the time I pull dirty dishes out of the dishwasher…rinse 'em off in the sink and the hell with the whole thing!
TOD:	Your problem is trifling—I had a big problem—somebody fell out of love with me.
BARNEY:	Blanche.
TOD:	Blanche. Before Blanche ran off with that corporate lawyer, I tried something but it didn't work. I guess it was too late.
BARNEY:	What was it, Tod?
TOD:	Blanche and I started to do the dishes together. She'd wash and I'd wipe. It was kinda relaxing. We even used to talk sometimes…once in a while…a couple of times. Somebody's battery needed changing. Not mine. We were just washing dishes.
BARNEY:	(*Understands*)…uh…Jane says the dishes have to be sterilized. Intense heat.
TOD:	We didn't have a dishwasher and there wasn't *any* heat, from her.
BARNEY:	Here's your beer. I was just holdin' it. It was gettin' warm.
TOD:	Good talk comes first. Thanks. (*Pause*)
BARNEY:	(*Chuckles*) Hey, why do you always say that Blanche ran away with a corporate lawyer? You're a hard guy to figure out!
TOD:	That's what I'd tell the neighbors. I figured it would make them feel that Blanche was getting a better deal out of life than bein' with me. It sounded nicer than sayin' my 'old lady' ran off with a bum!
BARNEY:	I never heard you call Blanche your 'old lady!'
TOD:	That's why I didn't wanna say it.
BARNEY:	Well, I know that this guy wasn't a corporate lawyer, but he wasn't a bum either, right?
TOD:	Sure he was! His toes were comin' out of his shoes…like in the cartoons…and he had a 'bag on a stick'…he smoked a cigar butt on a toothpick. He was a cliché um-bay!!
BARNEY:	(*Chuckle*)
TOD:	This bum would sling this 'bag on a stick' over his shoulder. He called it a 'Bindle'…he used to stuff his dental floss and toilet paper in it. He traveled the way bums travel…light. He hopped freights…oh, you know…the whole scenario!
BARNEY:	I get the picture! (*Chuckle*) But seein' is not believin'…When Blanche ran away with him, did he make her a 'bindle?'
TOD:	It would have been nice—but that information never filtered down

to me.

BARNEY:	You must have thought a lot of Blanche to tell a hokey story like that to the neighbors.
TOD:	Did I neglect to tell you that I adored that woman?...I'm still in love with her. Did I tell you that we used to do the dishes together.
BARNEY:	Yeh. That was really something, Tod!
TOD:	We only did it *once*. (*Beat*) I think we were on the right track, but we waited too long.
BARNEY:	Yeh.
TOD:	It was too late, Barney.
BARNEY:	I keep gettin' this idea, more and more, that Jane and I should do the dishes together. Anything to get her away from that damn dishwasher!
TOD:	I thought you said that she didn't really use it—that she didn't turn it on half the time!
BARNEY:	Yeh, I did say something like that. (*Thinks*) Maybe...maybe if I helped her load it—and learned to turn it on—and helped her take the dishes out.
TOD:	...and maybe, during this joint effort...your hands might touch.
BARNEY:	A kind of togetherness!
JANE:	(*Off*) Barney!
BARNEY:	(*Calls*) Yeh!
JANE:	(*Off*) Will you turn the dishwasher on? (*Beat*) I think it's prob'ly full enough.
BARNEY:	(*Calls*) I donno how to turn it on, Jane!
TOD:	Keep goin'!
BARNEY:	Why doncha come down and show me.
TOD:	I gotta go now, pal—but think about this—who was that 'un-masked man' who saved your marriage!! You can finish my beer!

[Nothing particularly dramatic happens in this scene. One of the goals is to make it sound real—natural while finding the subtle changes in what is being said so that there is some "movement" to it.]

EVERYTHING'S PATTERNS — EVEN WAFFLES
(2 Men, 1 Woman)

JOE:	Would you mind sitting at the counter?
BILL:	Huh?
JOE:	Would you mind sitting at the counter?
BILL:	Yes.
JOE:	I mean, it's just you, I figured you wouldn't mind. I mean, you're all alone.
BILL:	I've got phone numbers if I wanted to use 'em…they're around someplace…I don't have to be alone if I don't want to.
JOE:	…but I'm not. See, I'm with this girl, Her name's…
BILL:	(*Up*) You don't have to introduce me – it's not that kind of a situation. I can see you're with a friend.
SALLY:	Hi.
JOE:	She's my girlfriend
BILL:	Hi.
SALLY:	Hi.
JOE:	We'd like to sit together.
BILL:	You lucked out…there's two seats together at the counter. Somebody's just leaving.
JOE:	Sally wanted a booth.
BILL:	I told you, you didn't have to tell me her name!
SALLY:	(*Giggles*)
JOE:	She wanted a booth.
BILL:	So did I…I got one.
JOE:	You don't have to get smart about this!

BILL:	Why not? Don Adams built a whole career on it.
SALLY:	(*Giggles*)
JOE:	What's so funny?
SALLY:	What he said was funny…about Don Adams.
BILL:	There's some people over there in *that* booth…they're just leaving. Grab it.
JOE:	I'm not through with you yet.
BILL:	What's 'not to be through?'…You asked…in a very nice…civil way…if I'd relinquish my booth and I was adamant.
SALLY:	Let's grab *that* booth, like he said, Joe. It's just as good as his ole booth.
JOE:	O.K.
BILL:	I suppose you think I'm rude?
JOE:	You were making fun of us. I just asked you for a simple favor.
BILL:	…and I turned you down. You should have walked away from it. Why'd you belabor it?
SALLY:	He didn't mean to. It's just that we just got married and we're still cozy-conscious.
BILL:	'Cozy-conscious?'
SALLY:	We just moved to this town from San Jose. People are friendlier there. I guess we expected them to be friendly here.
BILL:	Was I unfriendly?
JOE:	(*Negative reaction*)
SALLY:	That booth's gone.
JOE:	Huh?
SALLY:	That booth's gone. Some other people took that booth.
BILL:	Would you like to share my booth? I'll just get on with this cross-word puzzle…and pretend I'm not listening to what you're saying.
SALLY:	You want to, Joe?
JOE:	Sure. (*They sit*) How long you gonna be?
BILL:	I haven't been served yet.
JOE:	I mean, you gonna eat and then leave…or are you gonna sit and work on your puzzle…afterwards?
BILL:	I dunno…I think I'll wing it. The puzzle's starting out hard. It may have to be abandoned. Happens sometimes.
SALLY:	Maybe it'll get easier as you go along.
BILL:	That's just as bad—the challenge is somewhere in there between.
JOE:	You order breakfast?

BILL:	Yeh. Short stack, scrambled pigs-brains and beer.
JOE:	Why do you always have to say something smart?
BILL:	Whatta ya mean, 'smart?'—that's the 'dumbest' breakfast I ever heard of!
SALLY:	(*Giggles*)
BILL:	Actually, I'm having a waffle.
JOE:	…and you haven't got it yet? Why should it take so long to get a waffle?
BILL:	Because they don't make waffles here…they had to send out for it. I'm a good customer. They do things like that for me.
SALLY:	(*Giggles*) Where do they have to send for it?
BILL:	I dunno. What do I know from waffles? I just laid the challenge on 'em—and they'll resolve it—a little waffle-research.
SALLY:	Like the challenge in your crossword puzzle. You complicate everything, don't you?
BILL:	As a general rule, yes…but there *are exceptions*…but mostly, not. (*Beat*) It varies.
SALLY:	Joe and I're on a diet.
BILL:	Who's Joe?
SALLY:	This is Joe.
BILL:	Hi.
SALLY:	What's your name?
BILL:	Bill.
SALLY:	Joe…Bill…and Sally.
JOE:	I wish that waitress'd get over here. I'm starved.
SALLY:	Joe and I only eat three meals a day…and Joe gets impatient when they don't come…one…two…three.
BILL:	You eat all three at once?
SALLY:	No…I mean 'one'…eat that one…then comes time for 'two'…eat that one…then…
BILL:	I get it, yeh! (*Change*) Whatta you mean, you and Joe only eat three meals a day?
SALLY:	Yeh, but we don't eat between meals…we don't cheat. Sometimes Joe doesn't even eat between bites.
JOE:	Sally! You're going on and on here!
BILL:	Whatta you mean, Joe doesn't eat between bites?
SALLY:	Nothing really! It doesn't make sense. I just thought it was funny…not 'eating between bites' I mean!

JOE:	(*Up*) I think this is your waffle coming!
BILL:	Yeh! (*Up*) Got my waffle, Clarisse? (*Pause*)
SALLY:	She didn't say anything…the waitress.
BILL:	Her name's Clarisse.
SALLY:	…she didn't say anything.
BILL:	She doesn't plant cotton either…but then, as they say, those who do…are soon forgotten.
SALLY:	(*Sings*) That ole mail-order waffle—it just keeps comin'…unannounced! (*Giggles*)
JOE:	'Mail-order' waffle?
SALLY:	…just came right out—seemed like a funny thing to say.
JOE:	She gonna bring you syrup…butter?
BILL:	I'm sure she will.
JOE:	She didn't stop to take our order.
BILL:	This isn't her station.
JOE:	Huh?
BILL:	She works at the other restaurant…where they hadda send to get the waffle…it's just down a few doors.
JOE:	…so Clarisse brought it over.
SALLY:	If you wanted a waffle…and you knew they didn't serve waffles in here…why didn't you go to the other restaurant?
BILL:	I usually do.
JOE:	If you had…we would have got your booth.
SALLY:	…but then we wouldn't have got to know each other.
JOE:	We know each other's first names.
BILL:	Then we're on a first-name-basis…that's what 'good' friends are…usually. (*Change*) You better be thinking about what you want, Sally…so when the waitress on this station does come over…you'll be ready.
SALLY:	I think I want a waffle.
JOE:	They don't serve waffles here.
SALLY:	Let's go to his waffle place. (*To Bill*) Why doncha just take your waffle with you and pay for it over there.
BILL:	Good idea. Let's go. I hope we can find a booth.
SALLY:	If we can't…we could sit at the counter. (*Up*) Boy! This Beverly Hills is really some place to live!! There's never a dumb moment!! Let's go!!

[Many of the characters in Daws' scripts are highly intelligent and articulate. This one features a teenager so smart, the adults can't figure her out.]

THERE ARE TEENAGERS...AND TEENAGERS
(2 Men, 1 Woman)

SIDNEY:	(*Annoyed*) So you finally got here! We were on time!
BRUCE:	Sorry...I was checking over some notes in the Penthouse.
SIDNEY:	The elevator was out of order?
BRUCE:	No. I jogged down. I didn't get my exercise in this morning.
SIDNEY:	You can't beat a ' shrink's' logic!...(*Change*) But I think you could have hustled a little bit. I made this appointment two weeks ago. You said you'd be completely in the clear today—no hassling for your expensive attention. Doctor Bruce Harbinger doesn't come cheap!!
BRUCE:	I told you this meeting would be a 'freebee'...remember? A kind of auditing. Get an idea of what my services are. I thought you wouldn't consider my price so exorbitant.
SIDNEY:	Then you admit your prices are exorbitant?
BRUCE:	I'm not admitting anything. (*Beat*) I was just trying to give you a break, that's all.
SIDNEY:	When an analyst gives anybody a break, that'll be the day.
BRUCE:	I don't like your attitude. If you don't approve of me...I could put you on to Toni Grant. We've got a sneering relationship. Just what do you want to see me about?
CATHY:	Lay it on him, Dad!!
SIDNEY:	I want you to talk to my daughter! See what's with her! Destroy the bad seed! (*Introduces his daughter*)...Cathy, this is Doctor Bruce Harbinger.
CATHY:	I know.
SIDNEY:	(*Remembers*) Of course you do! I've been talking to him.
CATHY:	For quite a while. You're very good at talking.

SIDNEY:	I didn't talk any longer than necessary.
CATHY:	That 'you' thought was necessary. I think Doctor Harbinger got the idea.
BRUCE:	I did indeed…Yes. The way I accepted this meeting and the reason for it…was that your father was concerned about your adolescence, and certain problems which might surface unnecessarily—if he didn't circumvent them early on in your entry into the adult world.
CATHY:	…what you mean is…*you* think that *he* thinks that I'm a bubble-head.
BRUCE:	In *so* many words, yes.
CATHY:	In *too* many words you mean. This whole discussion sounds like a 'redundant verbosity convention.' There are three words which represent your 'Great State of intellectual incoherence.' The words are 'blah, blah, blah!'
BRUCE:	(*Impressed*) This kid really comes on!
CATHY:	I just 'say it.'
SIDNEY:	Is she too far gone, Doc?
BRUCE:	Don't for God's sake call me 'Doc!' Call me 'Doctor' or Bruce—but don't call me 'Doc!!' (*Goes on*) In answer to your concerned parental question…Yes
SIDNEY:	Yes?
BRUCE:	Yes…even though I have had scant time to evaluate the psyche of Miss Cathy…(*Stop*)
CATHY:	(*Quickly*) Don't for God's sake call me 'Miss Cathy!!' This is beginning to sound like an unamusing parody of a Tennessee Williams play! I'm just 'Cathy.'
BRUCE:	Straight out.
CATHY:	Just 'Cathy.' Not 'Miss Cathy.'…skip the magnolias.
SIDNEY:	What do you mean, this sounds like an unamusing parody of Tennessee Williams? (*Beat*) Who's he? (*Beat*) What's a parody?
CATHY:	We're all going on and on about everything. We're not saying things straight out. We're embroidering.
BRUCE:	But you were 'straight out' when you said your name was just Cathy.
CATHY:	What is this? An instant replay?
BRUCE:	Don't be nasty. You should only be nasty when your father is laying down big bucks.
SIDNEY:	Let's get down to business here. Cathy isn't acting like a normal teenager. She's been going off the deep end even before she became a teenager.

BRUCE:	In what way? Teenagers are my specialty!
CATHY:	I'll bet! With the couch doing double duty.
BRUCE:	(*Ignores her*) What about music? Is music the most important part of her life?
SIDNEY:	Yes, dammit!! Music is all right…but it's the type of music she listens to. It's unnatural and unhealthy.
BRUCE:	(*Warily*)…be specific.
SIDNEY:	Beethoven! Beethoven, for God's sake!
CATHY:	Mozart.
SIDNEY:	(*Confused*) I thought you liked Beethoven?
CATHY:	I like Beethoven…but now I'm into Mozart…and Schubert. I've 'back-burnered' Scriabin. He'll be there if I need him.
BRUCE:	This is serious.
SIDNEY:	Do you understand now why I was worried?
BRUCE:	I certainly do. You didn't come to me a moment too soon.
CATHY:	I find great satisfaction in music—not as a form of entertainment…but as sort of an intellectual food that my mind demands. I am nourished by it.
SIDNEY:	She plays it all the time!
BRUCE:	She is in deep trouble sure enough. (*Change*) Tell me, Cathy…do you like to read? If you do, don't be afraid to admit it. (*Lays it out*) Do you like to read?
CATHY:	Passionately. It is the highest and most graphic form of intellectual communication.
BRUCE:	(*Disgust*) Intellectual?
SIDNEY:	(*Shivers*) Oh my God!! My poor baby!
BRUCE:	What you read…does it stimulate your imagination in the discovery of the obscene and its variants?
CATHY:	(*Up—sharp*) Do you mean…do I read dirty books?
BRUCE:	Not in so many words.
CATHY:	But it's what you mean in however many words it takes for you to say it. Let's not play any games here…I'm on to you and your tribe!
BRUCE:	(*Gently*) Tell me about it, Sidney. How did it all start?
SIDNEY:	(*Up—under control*) I found some books in her room. She wasn't trying to hide them, thank God…but they were there! She has no shame!
CATHY:	They were my books. You had no right to pry!
BRUCE:	(*Cagily*) What were some of the titles…the authors?

SIDNEY:	(*Embarrassed but determined*) Charles Dickens!
BRUCE:	(*Shocked*) Oh my God!! (*Goes on*)...and the title?
SIDNEY:	Do I have to say it?
BRUCE:	Say it!
CATHY:	Spit it out, Dad!
SIDNEY:	'Oliver Twist'...and she read 'David Copperfield'...*twice*!
BRUCE:	Go on!
SIDNEY:	She had Franz Kafka under her pillow! (*Sobs*)
BRUCE:	...and does that end this litany of shame?
SIDNEY:	No! There were others! Jane Austen! Edgar Allen Poe! (*Breaks down—sobs*) I can't say anymore! Don't make me!
BRUCE:	(*Strong*) *You must*! It is her shame...not yours! Who else!!??
SIDNEY:	(*Tragically*) 'Moby Dick' by...by...I can't say it!
BRUCE:	You must! Blurt it out—rid yourself of this...poison!!
SIDNEY:	'Moby Dick' by Herman Melville. (*Sobs*) She reads...biographies!
BRUCE:	(*Sadly*) Biographies? Are you positive?
SIDNEY:	*I said she did, didn't I?* (*Goes on*) There's more! She loves the ballet! Poetry! There is no end to her teenage abnormalities!! She's not like her friends. She doesn't 'do' drugs. She's never had to be 'dried out'...She only drinks 'Dr. Pepper' for God's sake!!
BRUCE:	(*Emotional*) Trust me, Sidney! I can make her well!
SIDNEY:	I'll pay whatever you ask! I'll mortgage my life if necessary!!
BRUCE:	I want nothing. This will be a holy and dedicated expression of my...and your...despair at her decadence!
CATHY:	Forget it, both of you! I'm doomed but I'm happy. So leave my psyche alone!!

[Whether performing this with voice only or adding body movements to it, the piece should sound like you are walking and seeing different things as you talk.]

A DOG LIKE ALICE
(1 Man, 2 Men or Women)

WALKER:	Good morning.
GUS:	Good morning.
WALKER:	You haven't got him with you today?
GUS:	He's a 'her.' No, I haven't.
WALKER:	Well, I've only noticed you from a distance. There seems to be a tendency to think of dogs as 'male' and cats as 'female.'
GUS:	It's a tendency?
WALKER:	Well, I mean—people *think that* for no reason.
GUS:	Anyway, Alice is a 'she.'
WALKER:	You haven't got her with you today. I've grown so used to seeing you two each morning…even at a distance, that I noticed her absence today.
GUS:	I don't know where she is.
WALKER:	You've been out looking for her?
GUS:	For a couple days now. I think she's gone.
WALKER:	Maybe she'll turn up. Animals do that, sometimes.
GUS:	Not Alice. I think she's gone. I'm worried about the medical lab at the University. They pick up animals for their experiments.
WALKER:	I've heard that—but I'm inclined to doubt it. They can't grab people's pets. (*Beat*) You're worried about it?
GUS:	Yes.
WALKER:	Why don't you go over to the lab and describe 'Alice' to them.
GUS:	If they was to grab her, I don't think they'd tell me about it. She's a German Shepherd—not too old and sometimes they have more trouble getting big dogs.

WALKER:	Well, let's romanticize it a bit. Maybe Alice will escape and find her own way home.
GUS:	No.
WALKER:	That doesn't sound like a possibility?
GUS:	No. Alice couldn't find her way home.
WALKER:	Why not?
GUS:	Because she's blind.
WALKER:	(*Beat*) Blind?
GUS:	I think somebody tried to do away with her when she was a pup. Looked like they threw acid on her. It didn't kill her but it did blind her. I found her in an alley, under some old trash. She was unconscious—and I took her on home and nursed her back to bein' alive at least.
WALKER:	How long ago was that?
GUS:	About two years. Since then I been keepin' her close to me—indoors—and only lettin' 'er out when we go for our daily walks.
WALKER:	Your life is pretty much centered in Alice, isn't it?
GUS:	The fun part of my life, yeh. I'm a sort of night watchman in that building over there. (*Points*) Not the big one—the little one next to it. It's a warehouse for text-books. Nothin' in there that anybody'd wanna steal, I got me a little room in there—a dinky stove. The best part is, I got me a toilet and a sink. I'm right proud of havin' as complete a place to live. I was blessed.
WALKER:	What do you do all day?
GUS:	Not much. I'm just supposed to be there…in the buildin'…
WALKER:	How do you occupy your time—your mind?
GUS:	I'm eighty-five years old. I don't have no past worth rememberin' and the future is sort of a tunnel…and I never even think about lookin' ahead to see if there's a light at the end of it. Even if there was, it wouldn't mean nothin.' Every day is about the same.
WALKER:	And you go for your walks with Alice.
GUS:	That's what I been doin', yeh. (*Sigh*) I got me a cane with a white tip. I have it with me when Alice and I take our walks. I got her on a leash—and folks, seein' us, think that I'm the one that's blind and Alice is my dog.
WALKER:	(*Thoughtfully*) What if you don't find Alice?
GUS:	I can't think that far ahead…I start to and then somethin' distracts me. I was goin' from day to day…now I kinda go from hour to hour. (*Remembers*) Alice and I used to go around back at the McDonald's hamburger place…and the young lady in

there…when she'd see me and Alice out there…she'd bring out parts of hamburgers that were left on the plate. She'd give 'em to me for Alice—but she knew I was gonna eat some too. Alice liked her. When she come out back, Alice would sense it—and she'd kind of quiver and move her sightless eyes to where the girl was talkin'…Alice loved to go to McDonald's.

WALKER: (*Sees something*) There's someone waving-coming over here from the lab. (*Calls*) You wanted to see us about something?

MAN/WOMAN: (*Comes on*) I'm from the University Lab. I think it's your dog we've found. We snatched her out of the middle of the street yesterday. We bathed her—gave her some shots she's probably been needing for a long time—and she's over there waiting for you—I didn't know where to call you—but we'd seen you out 'walking' her. We knew she belonged to you—and we'd spot you sooner or later.

GUS: Thank you.

MAN/WOMAN: We saw you with the cane—we thought you were blind—now we know it was the dog.

GUS: Thank you.

MAN/WOMAN: Come along over—and you can take your dog home.

GUS: Her name is Alice.

MAN/WOMAN: Alice is a nice name for a dog.

GUS: Thank you. I'll come with you. (*To Walker*) Thank you for your interest. I guess the tunnel did have a light after all.

[There is more going on here than a husband telling his wife about how he knows the waitress. The characters are not saying exactly what they mean here. It is up to you to dig deep beyond the surface of each person.]

INFIDELITY SPOKEN HERE
(1 Man, 2 Women)

(*Scene—a quiet restaurant. A man and his wife. A female 'table-hopper' speaks briefly—then 'hops' on*)

MARGY:	(*Recognition*) Andy! Andy Warner! Where were you yesterday? We missed you! Call me! Sorry to interrupt! (*Goes off*) Bye!
PATRICE:	What was that all about?
ANDY:	She's an actress.
PATRICE:	What's her name?
ANDY:	Margy. Margy Cooper.
PATRICK:	She said she missed you.
ANDY:	Not just her. She said…'we' miss you.
PATRICE:	…and who are 'we?'
ANDY:	They're a bunch of 'out of work' actors. They're in a play on Melrose.
PATRICE:	(*Beat*)…and?
ANDY:	…and Margy asked me if I would direct a little. They were in a bind. The director they had walked off. He got a job that paid money, I guess.
PATRICE:	How did 'Margy' know you were a director? On second thought, you're not a director.
ANDY:	(*Nettled*) I direct commercials.
PATRICE:	Forgive me!
ANDY:	Direction is direction. I write the drek and I suppose it just comes naturally for me to direct it.
PATRICE:	How'd she know you were such a 'hot-shot' director?

ANDY:	She did a spot for me a month or so ago. The thing had gone to three 'call-backs' and she ended up doing it.
PATRICE:	How many actresses were called back?
ANDY:	Just two. Margy and this other actress.
PATRICE:	Did she have a name?
ANDY:	Sure she had a name—but she didn't get the spot so what the hell's the difference?
PATRICE:	She was called back three times...she must have had something!
ANDY:	Not enough to nail down the spot!
PATRICE:	...and you don't even remember her name.
ANDY:	Sure I do. Her name was Bernice 'something.'
PATRICE:	Bernice didn't make much of an impression on you.
ANDY:	I guess not.
PATRICE:	Let's get back to this directing 'thing.' You said Margy got the spot.
ANDY:	Right, and she was damn good! National spot...oughta pay her rent for a while.
PATRICE:	...and you directed the session?
ANDY:	I always direct my sessions.
PATRICE:	How'd you come to direct the play Margy was in?
ANDY:	You don't listen! They had a director, but I guess he was no great shakes. He walked out. Left them high and dry.
PATRICE:	...so you took over?
ANDY:	Right! The 'thing''s been running a couple weeks now.
PATRICE:	And you got acquainted with Margy and the cast?
ANDY:	Yeh. They appreciated the fact that I jumped in and pulled things together.
PATRICE:	...and now they miss you?
ANDY:	That's what Margy said.
PATRICE:	(*Thoughtful*) I wonder who misses you the most.
ANDY:	I guess they all miss me the same. I directed all of 'em.
PATRICE:	It's nice to be missed. (*Beat*) Any love scenes in the play?
ANDY:	One. There was one.
PATRICK:	...and I'll bet that Margy was in it!
ANDY:	Right.
PATRICE:	She have any trouble doing it?
ANDY:	Yeh. The kiss. She didn't show enough abandon in the embrace.

PATRICE:	I see. So you kept her after rehearsal.
ANDY:	I did, yeh. I spent a little time with her in the Green Room.
PATRICE:	I suppose this was after the rest of the cast had gone home…
ANDY:	I didn't want to embarrass her. She finally got the idea.
PATRICE:	I'll bet! Good for little Margy! But this doesn't surprise me. You've always had a soft spot in your head for 'calculated vulnerability'…did you send out for 'Chinese' afterwards?
ANDY:	What?
PATRICE:	One does experience hunger 'afterwards'…
ANDY:	This is nonsense! Don't get any ideas!!
PATRICK:	I just hope you didn't get any ideas…
ANDY:	…about Margy and I?
PATRICE:	No. About Margaret Thatcher and you.
ANDY:	Listen, Patrice—if there were any ideas? I'd have had 'em by now!
PATRICE:	Have you? (*Beat*) Had 'em?
ANDY:	(*Stumbles*) In…in a way.
PATRICE:	I'm confused. That is not a precise, definite, *strong* answer.
ANDY:	Look, I give my words the weight they need! I don't silicone 'em like you!
PATRICE:	Let my curiosity race ahead. (*Beat*) Did you sleep with her?
ANDY:	No!
PATRICE:	No?
ANDY:	No! (*Beat*) Not the first time! I…I just coached her.
PATRICE:	…but the second time you 'couched' her? Is that right?
ANDY:	(*Straight out—trapped*) Yeh! That's right! (*Big change. Alarm*) What's she coming back for? It's Margy!
MARGY:	(*Comes on*) Andy! I was waiting for you outside. (*To Patrice*) I didn't mean to be rude before. I just sort of barged in on you. I wouldn't have done that a few years ago—but Andy's taught me to be myself—to do what comes naturally!
PATRICE:	I know.
MARGY:	You know?
PATRICE:	Andy's told me a lot about you.
MARGY:	(*Enthused*) Are you one of Andy's clients? I worked for Andy!
PATRICE:	(*Dryly*) I guess one can make 'work' out of anything.
MARGY:	How do you mean?
ANDY:	(*Urgent*) Knock it off, will ya, Patrice. Let me handle this!

PATRICE:	…you already have!
MARGY:	(*Up*) *Are* you one of Andy's clients?
PATRICE:	I'm his wife.
MARGY:	I thought maybe you were a client.
PATRICE:	I'm his wife.
MARGY:	His wife! (*Thinks*) He didn't tell me he was married. (*Beat*) Isn't that strange?
PATRICE:	Yes, it is. It's as strange as finding vegetables in vegetable soup.
MARGY:	(*Quickly*) But there *are* vegetables in vegetable soup!
PATRICE:	Then maybe it's not so strange.
ANDY:	(*Through his teeth*) Lay off, Patrice! This is embarrassing!
PATRICE:	(*To Margy*) Andy doesn't like embarrassing situations for you, Margy.
MARGY:	I know! Isn't that sweet? I was in an embarrassing situation in this play I'm in.
PATRICE:	…and Andy helped you.
MARGY:	I didn't know how to kiss—and Andy helped me.
PATRICE:	(*Quickly*) He helped himself and you were the entree.
MARGY:	What?
PATRICE:	Andy told me that you two have slept together.
MARGY:	That's not true!
PATRICE:	You're calling my husband a liar?
MARGY:	After Andy and I made love I got dressed and went home!
ANDY:	(*Beaten down*) Oh my God!
MARGY:	(*Chirpy*) Later that night I went to sleep though!
ANDY:	Let's get the hell out of here!
MARGY:	Do you know what I'm like? I'm like Peter Sellers in that movie 'BEING THERE.'
PATRICE:	You are?
MARGY:	Yes, but there's a difference. He liked to 'watch'…and I like to 'do!'
PATRICE:	But you only do it with Andy?
MARGY:	Only with Andy!…Andy is my one and only! (*Puzzled*) I thought if you knew about this…you'd be mad.
PATRICE:	A while back, I might have been. I've been considering a divorce. I just finished my Spring cleaning and maybe I'll make it a 'clean sweep.'
MARGY:	I'm sorry.

PATRICE:	Don't be—it won't be a messy divorce, Andy and I will always be friends.
MARGY:	I'm glad!
PATRICE:	I'm just glad that I had the chance to experience you, Margy. You're so honest.
MARGY:	Like Abe. Lincoln, I mean.
PATRICE:	I guessed that. No Margy—as far as I'm concerned, you can sleep with Andy as much as you please.
MARGY:	Thank you, Patrice! (*Quickly*) But there is one thing! I've got workshops on Tuesday and Thursday. (*Up*) Well, I've gotta run along now! Thanks for Andy!!
PATRICE:	(*Beat*) Andy…
ANDY:	(*Weakly*) Yes.
PATRICE:	I take back the line about 'calculated vulnerability!'

[Approach this piece from the perspective that each character has a different view of sex and use it to color how the lines are said. One sobs at the thought of it. One is flip about it and one is indifferent to it.]

TELLING IT LIKE IT IS
("MORE MAJESTY")
(3 Women)

MAJESTY:	All right, Myra...what's it all about? I got the call about Florence.
MYRA:	She's upstairs. I just dropped by to look at her new needlepoint...it's incredible. Those original designs.
MAJESTY:	What's the problem?
MYRA:	Why does everything have to be a problem with you?
MAJESTY:	Knock it off, Myra. You came on pretty heavy...I left a meeting! Margaret's Lew Tarkman was presenting some research data...
MYRA:	Florence is in shock.
MAJESTY:	Over what?
MYRA:	She suddenly became aware...of something that had never occurred to her before.
MAJESTY:	You're not telling me anything!
MYRA:	Go upstairs. You talk to her.
MAJESTY:	Her sainted Aunt Myra...
MYRA:	Go to hell!
MAJESTY:	Her 'sainted' Aunt Myra couldn't cut it? Florence turned off? No charisma?
MYRA:	Cool it, Majesty...let's both go up. (*Change*) O God! She's coming down!
FLORENCE:	(*Coming on*) Mama! Aunt Myra! (*Sobs*)
MAJESTY:	I'm here, Florence...what's wrong? Tell me.
FLORENCE:	How can I?
MYRA:	Tell her, sweetheart...you told me.
FLORENCE:	(*Sobs*) It's Benny.

MAJESTY:	(*Annoyed*) Benny? What'd Benny do now?
MYRA:	He didn't 'do' anything. (*Pause*) It's all right, Florence...tell your mother what you told me...
MAJESTY:	Then she *did* tell you something?
MYRA:	Go on, Florence.
FLORENCE:	Well...mama...you chewed Benny out because his room was so messy. It's always messy...but you were so mad this morning...so when Benny went out, I thought I'd clean up his room (*Sobs*)...and...under the bed...I found...(*Sobs*)
MYRA:	Go on, Florence...
FLORENCE:	I found those...magazines... (*Sobs*)
MAJESTY:	(*Quietly*) Magazines.
MYRA:	*Those* magazines.
MAJESTY:	(*Quietly*) O God!
FLORENCE:	...the pictures!!
MAJESTY:	O Florence! You poor darling.
FLORENCE:	There were so many! Why did Benny...
MYRA:	Florence. You and Benny have always been close. You love each other. You've shared so many things over the years...but Benny— Benny couldn't share with you...something that's...O God!...
MAJESTY:	Macho.
MYRA:	That's right, Benny's growing up...pretty soon, he'll be a man...
FLORENCE:	(*Reacts*) But those...pictures!
MAJESTY:	Benny is going through a very painful transition. He's suddenly aware of himself...and of his desires.
FLORENCE:	But those...'women!'
MAJESTY:	Florence...Benny doesn't relate to 'those' women...yet. He's relating to the fact that they *are* 'women.' He feels a desire for...
MYRA:	It's really not that terrible, Florence. All boys feel this way...Benny is just another assembly-line product...
FLORENCE:	You mean...he wants to...
MAJESTY:	He's considering it...
MYRA:	He's thinking about it...it's nothing out of the ordinary, Florence...Benny is just realizing what being a man is all about...
FLORENCE:	Those magazines...under the bed. Where anybody—(*Up*) Where *I* found them...
MAJESTY:	But it was *Benny's* room. 'His' room...messy, sloppy...whatever. I did get after him about it. I know that. But it was his

room...to keep the way he wanted it. If he wanted to live in a slum, so be it!

MYRA: The last thing in the world he would have expected, was to have you...or anyone...investigate the under-side of his bed.

FLORENCE: ...but I was cleaning up...I didn't know...

MYRA: Well, you know now...

FLORENCE: (*Plosive sigh*)

MYRA: You have also learned something about boys...

MAJESTY: Don't let Benny know about your finding the magazines. He loves you, Florence...he wouldn't want you to think less of him...not that you should.

FLORENCE: Why didn't he talk to Daddy?

MAJESTY: Why didn't he talk to Daddy. (*Up*) O God! The rationale cop-out. It just doesn't work that way, Florence. Time and tide and puberty wait for no man...and especially...boy-man...the answer has gotta be now. Talking to Daddy'd make as much sense as rolling a snow-ball back 'up' the hill until its a snow-flake. (*Up*) O boy! A snow-flake—the beginning!

MYRA: But the snow-ball is here...now. It exists. It's a culmination. The 'why' is ancient history. Benny has discovered sex...

MAJESTY: Au contraire! Sex has discovered Benny...poor, little, unsuspecting Benny.

FLORENCE: Don't make a joke out of it!

MYRA: But it is a joke, darling. Sex is God's punch-line. *Sex* and love...for some people (necessarily in that order)...is what it's all about. Y'see, men invented work, art, science...war. But they're all distractions.

FLORENCE: What about *love* and sex?

MAJESTY: Still on the drawing board. For many women, sex is like liver'n'onions...they'd never order it, but if somebody serves it, they find it most pleasant...and wonder why they don't have it more often...

MYRA: There are in-born compensations when it comes to sex...or the lack of it. If you're underweight or undersexed...don't knock it! You may be missing something but if you're not sure what it is— what difference does it make?

MAJESTY: Just remember this. Your first love affair should be with yourself...know, like, love and understand yourself and if you can work it in...respecting yourself ain't bad.

MYRA: In the beginning, after all the galaxies exploded and did their thing...and the world 'was'...the question came up. God tried to 'table' it...but was voted down.

FLORENCE:	(*With it now*) By whom?
MAJESTY:	Who remembers committees? Go on, Myra.
MYRA:	The question came up—'what you gonna do with all this real estate?'
FLORENCE:	(*Still with it*) 'Who' asked the question?
MYRA:	I was ready for that, darling...if God could create the world...
MAJESTY:	...and committees...
MYRA:	...he could certainly create a convenient straight-man...
MAJESTY:	Maybe Adam was a rub-off...
MYRA:	Had to be! Then God got a girl to join Adam's act.
MAJESTY:	...and then you know what he did? He knocked out the strongest and the longest running story-line of all time...it went through...and it's still going through endless re-writes...
MYRA:	But the punch-line is always the same...sex.
MAJESTY:	...and the straight-man got his answer. (*Change—softly*) Florence...don't think we're trite.
FLORENCE:	But you are trite.
MYRA:	But don't think it...say it.
FLORENCE:	I just did!
MAJESTY:	That...is the point. It's the same thing with sex. Admit it exists. It does. It's like the dessert in a cafeteria...its always at the end of the line...
FLORENCE:	It is! I remember.
MAJESTY:	...it's always at the end of the line...right before you pay up...the dessert looks so good...and you say 'I really shouldn't!'
MYRA:	...but you do. You see, little Florence, God gives you strength for the game of life...but his hold-card...his winning card is...sex.
MAJESTY:	God plays a winning game...and the lamp is always lit...and the chairs are filled...
MYRA:	...and the agony of sex is our fear of it. It's like a crooked wheel in Vegas. We know what we can lose...but we keep playing...trying to find a straight casino.
MAJESTY:	We're not just wrapping up a neat little package for you, Florence... we're just playing with our favorite toys again...
FLORENCE:	I know...words. That's all this family's all about.
MAJESTY:	Look at it this way, Florence. Benny's finally got to the dessert...and all the good, wholesome things he's had up to now along the ole cafeteria trail...they've got to help him decide what he's gonna do with all the goodies....

MYRA: ...and he'll probably do what every young heterosexual does. He'll long for...and according to his conscience...he'll get someone to love and care for...and who won't look anything like one of those pictures in the magazine...

MAJESTY: She may be some mousy little female with no bosom and skinny legs...but he'll love her and cherish her...

MYRA: ...and she'll love and cherish him. Do you understand what we've been trying to say, Florence. About boys?

FLORENCE: I've always understood about other boys feeling 'that' way...but I never thought about Benny feeling that way...

MAJESTY: Accept it, Florence, Benny feels that way. (*Big change*) Why don't you go and make the salad for dinner?

FLORENCE: O.K. You want kidney beans?

MAJESTY: Up to you. You make the salad.

FLORENCE: I'll surprise you. (*Pause*)

MYRA: Well...we brought it off, Majesty.

MAJESTY: I don't think we've ever been together in one room...for this long, Myra. (*Throw-away*) I'm going upstairs...tell Florence we don't have any kidney beans...That'll be her second disappointment today.

MYRA: I will...your majesty! (*Both laugh*)

[Daws wrote these for a combination booklet and audio tape set in order to give students an overview of the various dialects voice actors may be called upon to master. Study the rhythm and phonetics of the words, and practice, practice, practice. A compact disc of Daws reading these can be ordered from the back of this book.]

How To Do Dialects

BRITISH

Y'know, the most extraordinary thing happened today. I was cleaning out my desk and I found the penknife I accused Damien of stealing...remember? Damien never admitted stealing it, of course, but I believed him to be lying. I never liked Damien. The knife gave me a good reason for my attitude. It was a valuable knife, I was never particularly fond of it—it was just that Uncle Dorset gave it to me and not him. Well, Susan, I'm glad now your judgment prevailed and I went to Damien's funeral.

* * *

If creativity is the prerogative, then celebrate, in song and story, the sustenance the muse will bring...the mental manna that affixes itself like mucilage to the mind of the privileged—to be translated later to the starving psyches of the forthright but unfeeling, non-cerebral, finite minds of the multitudes.

* * *

I would like to request that the first three rows kindly move back...because I have a tendency to flail my arms about when reciting vigorous poetry. In this way, there will be no injuries and no lawsuits.

GLADSTONE: Oh, dear, dear Miriamne! Let's just sit here. What did you want to tell me?

MIRIAMNE: Simply this, Gladstone. I know that you don't love me anymore.

GLADSTONE: Hard cheese, old girl!

MIRIAMNE: ...but I shall continue to love you.

GLADSTONE: Well, that's understandable, certainly!

MIRIAMNE:	It wasn't easy, loving you, Gladstone…but now that I've learned how, I grow nauseous at the thought of going through all that dreariness with some 'new' person.
GLADSTONE:	Oh, Miriamne…you're so sweet…so brave…and deliciously sentimental!
MIRIAMNE:	Yes…and you ain't getting none of my money!

* * *

Everything I've said, the clumsy jumble of words…is of no importance whatever. I spoke the words…but they had no meaning. I'm an empty-headed person. I've tried to appear otherwise…and with some success. There are those who think me learned…and do you know why? No one really listens.

* * *

COCKNEY

'ere! What you doin'? I got me fish'n'chips an' me pint'o'bitter an' now I needs me a place to sit whilst I puts 'em away! This 'ere's my place! Get away! Pushin' an' shovin'…yer no better'n me! Yer jist a clod o' clay…an' when the last breath goes outta ya, they kin fork ya down wi' the rest o' the mulch! – an' ye'll make the pritty flowers grow! – an' fer once, ye'll serve some purpose in life. Now you clear out, or I'll make a nice puddin' outta yer face!

* * *

We was all sittin' aroun' t'other night, havin' us a pint o'bitter…an' you lot knows 'ow I likes to twist things about sometimes…so we was sittin' there talkin'…an' my frien' Raoul walks in…I said "Raoul – t'other night I was watchin' TV Savalas on the Telly!" – 'e laughed at that, Raoul did—but 'e said "You got it all twisted about—what you mean, was you saw Telly Savalas on the TV!" I said "That's the whole point, Raoul—I twisted it about on purpose! That's why you laughed!" (*Thoughtful*) I donno about Raoul – e's my bes' frien'n'all—but 'e's not too clever up 'ere!

IRISH

I try to do what I can…what I can, I try to do…I do what I can to try. Sometimes, I get so busy, doin' inside out, what I should be doin' outside in…that I forget to do what I already did!

* * *

…t'other side of the glade is where they're makin' the movie…the widow Boyle's tiny scrap of land. Payin' 'er a tidy sum fer a place to put their equipment is what I heard. The ones who're payin' for it all is Guinness Stout…"The Facets of the Emerald" the movie'll be called—they want to git more Yanks over here with their 'hard cash' is what it's all about!…Y'see, there's a mist that comes into the glade, early mornin'…an' lays there like…it's a 'texture-shot' I heard one of them workin'-on-the-movie fellers say. Atmosphere, they're after—and the widow Boyle's great lummox of a son'll be after cajolin' whiskey money out've 'er! (*Up*) Aye! She'll hold the money in her dear little hand for so short a time, her fingers'll be touchin' 'fingers' again soon enough! — Shall we go up an' watch 'em then?

* * *

SCOTS

It's a pity you can't sympathize with a person that's afraid of the opposite sex—and not ashamed of it, either! It's all very well for you to poo-poo my fears, but there's no doubt about it—there's no more perfect coward in the wide world than me – and when I feel the hot breath of love comin' closer…I go home to my father and mother's farm—and the very first thing I do when I get in the house is to turn out the light and cower there in the dark—down on the floor with the lint and the wee, crawly beasties that live in the baseboard…and I cannot complain about their company—I prefer them—to the love-bug!!

* * *

PHONETIC (for Scots)

It's a pi-ee ya can't sympa*thize* wi' a pairson tha's afraid o' tha opposite sex—an' nah ashamed of it, either! It's ah vera wheel fer ye to poo-poo me fears, but there's nah doot aboot it—there's nah mair pairfect coward i' tha wide world than me—an' when I feel tha hot breath o' love coomin' closer—I gang hame r'me faither'n'maither's far-um—an' tha vera fairst thing I do when I ge' in the hoose is to tairn oot the licked an' cower there i' tha dark—doon on the floor wi' tha lint an' tha wee, crawly beasties tha' live i' tha baseboard—an' I canna complain aboot their coompany—I prefair them—to tha love-boog!!

ITALIAN

My wife made the pasta—your wife made the salad. The pasta is all gone—but there's tubs full of salad!!

* * *

My name is Michaelangelo—I'm a busy man! Where's the girl gonna pose for my painting? You—Mona Lisa! C'mere! You got a 'call-back,' right? Siddown. It's time for lunch but I gonna squeeze you in, do a 'quickie'—now—gimme nice big smile. (*Pause*) Nice big smile. (*Pause*) Open your face! (*Up*) What's the matter, you not gonna give me nice, big smile? Who's got time for this?!!—I'm gonna send you to Leonardo di Vinci! – he needs the work!!

****

It's a little slow, Rose—so you fill the sugars—I'll get the napkins. (*Pause*) The lousy rain! I din feel like goin' out las' night, so I watch on the TV, KOJAC! That big guy!…Everybody says the bald head, it's sexy, y'know? To me, in his voice, it's the music! I get his vibes, y'know?—but you turn down the sound an' jus' look at the picture an' whatta ya see? What yer lookin' at, is this big guy—he could be a fry-cook!!

* * *

BROOKLYN

Will you listen to me? Come here!—Now, just stand there – just stand there! (*Breath expulsion*) Naw, I don't want no coffee. I want to explain…something, uh…I want to explain something to you, already…Look, I sort of intended to call you on the phone the other day, y'know? Then I says…uh…"Why bother?" (*Beat*) Naw, I don't mind paying for no lousy phone call!—but I figure like…uh…I was going to see you today on that matter, y'know?…and not only that, but uh…(*Light chuckle*) when 'you' get on the phone, you talk too much! (*Up*) You want the truth? You're a talker!—you don't know that, huh? (*Slight derisive sound*) My father, he always says…uh…"talk is cheap," y'know?…yeh, well, my time ain't, see?—That's the way it goes!…insulted? (*Dry chuckle*) What insulted? You talk too much! You want to know why?—huh?—'cause 'you' got a tendency…for redundant!—'Once' you can't say some-thing—you've got to…yakkity-yak all over the place! Who's got time for that? Anyway, here we are. I'm here. You're here. (*Up*) O.K. so if I insulted you…so be insulted, already! – and…uh…go get the money from some…uh…some other jerk!

* * *

HINDU

Ah…denk you…denk you very much! I am very glod do hev de obbordunidy of comin' 'ere. You zee, ven I dalk…like de Indian…id iz imbossible…imbossible for me to zay 'imbossible' – because I cannod zay 'p'—an' very difficuld for me do zay 't'…zo I mus' exblain dose bardicular vords! O yes! O yes indeed, indeed yes! O my yes!…ve hev a lod of beoble, you know. In India…and, indeed, in Bakisdan, who are loveen do listen do da 'sdandub' comedians — an' zomeday, I vould love do go do Los Angeles…an' go do da 'comedy-sdore' an' dell zome of my jokes!! (*Slight chuckle*) Here in India, I ged gread lahffs ven I dell my jokes…beoble find id very difficuld to maindain dere combosure ven I zay dees funny dings!—I call dem, my 'pun-jabs!'…led me give you an exomble!! (*Clears throat*) Ladely, I hev been very busy…O yes indeed! Led me dell you how busy I vas….I vas as busy as a mongoose ad a cobra-rally! (*Laughs*) I find id difficuld do maindain my combosure! (*Laughs*) I hobe you vere able to maindain yours! (*Laughs*) Bud nod do much!!!

* * *

GERMAN

I am Ludvig Van Beethoven. My whole life iss music—morning, noon und night—music, music, music. (*Beat*) Music!! (*Pause*) *I like music!* (*Throw-away*) Once in a vhile, a liddle schnapps! — my whole, my entire life vas music. I neffer vent to da Chunior Prom…I neffer 'plate' no schtoop-tag…no schtick-ball. In dose days, dere vasn't no residuals—you ge-knocked oud a tune…you got da 'bret'…und dot vas it! Close da door on da vay oud, Charlie! Come back ven you god anudder vinner! (*New thought*) Vun day, I vas valkin' down da street an' I see dis guy, Murray. He vas a Duke—He took hisself very serious — nod too many laughs vit dis guy. He had a tendency to patronize people. (*Up*) Thank God!! — so he said to me, he said: "Wolfgang!"…he alzo had very bad eyes!…he said: "How'd you like to pick up zum extra bret, playin' a schwingin' gig at my place, Saturday night?" I said: "I'll be dere—C-Sharp!…I mean, Eight Sharp—an' I'll bring already a new tune!" — so I qvick ge-knock out dis sonata, vich turned oud to be a *tremendous—a socko*! (*Throw-away*) It vas pretty good. (*Goes on*) Anyvays, because I vas gonna make it zum extra bret vit dis turkey, I called it "THE MOON-LIGHTER'S SONATA!!"

* * *

FRENCH

FORMS OF ADDRESS

Monsieur—MUH-*SUUUR*	Messieurs—*MAY*-SUUUR
Madam—MUH-*DAHM*	Mesdames—*MAY*-DAHM
Mademoiselle – MAD-MWAH-ZELL	Mesdemoiselles – *MADE*-MWAH-ZELL

The United States. My being here. What to talk about? There are so many things. I remember, in Paris, strolling down the Champs Elysses, at that time, my favorite boulevard — but now, there is Wilshire Boulevard! I may go to Bullocks, the Broadway, the May Company—these terrific department stores! But do I go there? No! Because of my inherent French frugality, I go to Fedco!…now, what else do I notice? With your permission, I will supply another example. As I sit here in my apartment, I realize that even when I was very young, I was positive that I would discover in the world…and I did!…the combination of comedy and tragedy…the actualities that were then only romantic dreams—a figment of my imagination. Fortunately, and perhaps because I was at an age when I…in a crowd with others…instead of wanting to disappear in thin air from embarrassment…I desired, more than anything, to be accountable for any possible difference in the international Dance of Life—this was to me, desirable…a giant-st in my maturity—and the truth of the matter is…I looked forward to having a bon appetite—having on the table, for my supper, Colonel Sanders Kentucky Fried Chicken—and from the House of Pies, Boyzenberry ala mode! Or, as we new American French say…boyzenberry, underneath ice-cream, please!!

* * *

AMERICAN SOUTHERN

Folks ask me if I like grits. Well, I like grits a lil bit—jist a lil bit. (*Up*) There is no mark on a ruler…small enough to show…how much I like grits…but I like grits a lil bit!

* * *

Dorthea…Dorthea! I want to ask you something…uh…no, no, no…I want to tell you something! I am going to come by your place, this afternoon…an' we're going fishing. (*Beat*) We're going fishing, I said! (*Up*) I'll bait us up—you jist set there and watch that bobbin! (*Beat*) Dorthea…listen. Every guy in town, is jist so jealous of me – 'cause they think you is the prettiest thing…and you are! But you're no fun! (*Beat*) Kissing? (*Chuckle*) I only kissed you once…took me three weeks to get up nerve and you dint do that very good! You got so uptight when you knew what I was about to do, you swung your face around and I almost kissed your nose! (*Beat*) Well, kissing ain't all that much fun anyhow—fishing is! (*Lays it out*) So we're going fishing! You be ready, hear? And I'll get you a Big Mac on the way home.

* * *

Hey, Marthy! (*Chuckle*) Mary-Ellen Forbush come by, looking for Daniel-Edmund…yeh, he done took her car in to the transmission place to have it fixed…got the keys from Mary-Ellen's mama. Yeh, well, Mary-Ellen Forbush, you know, she was right peevish about it. She's on that women's lib — well, maybe Daniel-Edmund should have let Mary-Ellen Forbush take her own car in! Them transmission people, they like a woman to come in with her own car! She don't need no men-folk to do for her! (*Dry chuckle*) But it would hurt Daniel-Edmund's feelings. He like to do for Mary-Ellen Forbush…he a proper man. He just ain't the type to take this here women's lib lip!

* * *

Now, let's see—it wasn't until the twelfth century (I think it was on a Thursday) that dust was discovered.

* * *

The Aardvark, regardless of what you may have heard to the contrary, was ferreted out and captured by a small boy, not in the interest of science, but as a personal favor to a Mr. Webster—who was writing a dictionary at the time, and needed words desperately to fill up the first page. Now, if you don't believe me—you can look it up!

* * *

When I was a kid, I was poor. I remember when I was hungry, I used to go next door and ask the lady for a piece of bread…'course, I always asked for French-toast and molasses…I was poor, but I was proud!

[The key to this piece is the subtext. On the surface, the character is all bravado but there is a real, feeling person underneath. It is for the actor to decide what the subtext is. Use the (Changes) *to play with different directions his/her moods and thoughts can go in.]*

THE AGENT
(Man or Woman)

Siddown, Honey...I remember your name...you don' hafta tell me...I called you back, remember?—Everybody loved your test...I meant to call ya, but I was busy (the goddam phone!)...I apologize for that...(*Change*) What apologize? You're the one who wants somethin' from me, right?...Don' look like that, Maria...I say things straight out...I come on strong maybe...but I'm a pussy-cat! I'm like Don Rickles, but *I* tell ya at the *beginnin'* of my act. (*Change*) Yeh, it was about some pain-in-the-ass...I hadda get over there and explain a few things. (This guy is scoring, God knows why, but mentally, he's not toilet-trained...an' he turned off a lot of important people...(*Throw away*) How he ever got booked at the Governor's Ball is...(*Change*)...but that's not your problem...Anyway, I'm glad to see you again. (*Up*) Everybody loved your test, I tell you that? (*Change*) You wanna know somethin', Maria...you're me...six, seven...O.K. twenty years ago! (O Christ! to be underweight again!)...I realize times are tough, but as far as I'm concerned, bein' poor is a cop-out and you get no credit for bein' a size seven. (*Change*) My boss doesn't know it yet, but we're gonna make a bundle on you...we get so few naturals in here, I'm gonna give it to ya straight...Maria, don' change a goddam thing! (*Up*) If I ever catch you in a girdle!!...Look, Maria...when you walk, you've got a tick-tock-tuchis...that'd turn the head of a Monsigneur!! Even if he was dozin', he'd 'twitch!' (*Up*) What sacrilegious? It's the way I talk...it don' mean nothin'...I make a point, right? You got no doubts, you know what I'm talkin' about, right?...right! (*Change*) What you are...you are a baby-doll...a love object (without sex!)...what I'm tryin' to tell ya, people are hard up for 'caring'...they need you! You're chocolate, without calories...you're everybody's dream! You're a natural as I wish my hair was. With your talent, all you need is me...to whisk off home-plate so's you can go to bat for the whole world!...and for you, I'm gonna put 'heart-break' on 'hold'...(maybe I'll even yank the cord outta the wall! (*Change*) Maria...listen to me. You act from your gut, and you got eyes that 'honest to God' climb inside of people...an' rearrange all their personal furniture! You make 'em see life the way it *could be*!...You got somethin' precious to sell, darlin'. (*Up*) Not your body, for God's sake!...What you've got, it's that formless, fabulous 'somethin'' that's...you! A guy...any guy...can see you...close his eyes and you're still there...see what I'm drivin' at? (*Change*) Look, when you've got somethin', an' you know (no bull-pippy) that it's special! (*Searches*) I mean…if Christ was livin' today…with the beautiful 'package-deal' for salvation he came up with…*he'd take out an ad in Variety!!* (*Change*) Don' look like that!! I'm not sacrilegious! I talk the way I talk—I am strictly a first-draft (I got no time for re-writes!). You better learn to love me for the way I am, sweetheart!… To me, you could be just another client…but you got the unfair advantage of bein' a human bein'…and for this ole girl [or guy], that's a first!! (*Change*) You're smilin', Maria!…We're gonna be friends, I'm really glad you finally got to me. I remember, you walked into the office…you said, 'I got talent.' I said, 'Whatta you do?' You said, 'Whatta want me to do…I've got it all!' Not exactly heavy dialogue…but you got through to me…(*Up*) Listen, Maria…you're the only person…when I say you're 'viable'…I know, for God's sake, once…what viable means!!

[This is an exercise in the New York dialect. But it is also about how to make the mundane interesting. It can be played many ways and is open to the actor's interpretation. Does he really believe his life is exciting or is he trying to convince himself of it? Or is he just making idle conversation?]

NEW YORKER
(Man)

What I did, I walked to work as usual this mornin' (I work over on Thirty-Third street) I got no car or motor-bike or nothin' like that, y'know—an' I don' work out no more like I usta, so you wanna know somethin'?—I could use the exercise! (*Beat*) I get to the store an' reach in my pocket for the key (I'm supposed to open up) but the key wasn't there! (*Beat*) What I did, I forgot the .key. I was perplexed, bothered and bewildered, like the song on one of them Oldies but Goodies albums they advertise on the TV allatime, y'know? But I don' dig music that much, so I never sent for this album. What turns me on is bowlin' an' snooker an' with them two great sports, I get to meet jokers with similar-type interests to what I got—which is somethin' when you got a dumb job you hate – an' you can't even do the dumb job 'cuz ya forgot the lousy key! (*Change*) What a routine I got—eat, sleep, work—I don' even go out much, (*Up*) There was this chick, y'know—I used to go for her. She was gung-ho on your rock'n'roll an' alla time I hadda take her to them rock concerts. I took this particular chick to five concerts way the hell out in Queens and all over the place. What happened I got mugged three times after I took her home—them ain't my type percentages so I dropped her (and anyways, every time I called her up she was busy, so I'm glad I dropped her!)…I suppose you're wonderin' what happened to the key an' all, huh? What else? I walked home an' got it—walked back—opened up and did my dumb job. (*Beat*) That's why Paul Newman hates me—I got this here excitin' life-style!

[This piece can be played with other actors who remain silent or alone while imagining the other characters are there. Note the many parenthetical directions. In most scripts, they are merely suggestions. Here they are a part of the exercise. They should be played exactly as written. This piece is about the timing between the lines more than the lines themselves.]

A BAD TIME WAS HAD BY ALL
(Man)

This is the traumatic conclusion of what has been a disastrous visit by IN-LAWS from the MIDWEST. The brother and nephew are taking the relatives to the LOS ANGELES AIRPORT to see them off.

THE CAR PULLS IN AT THE AIRPORT—LON, THE NEPHEW, IS DRIVING. HIS FATHER SPEAKS:

FATHER: There's a place to park over there! (*Annoyed*) Lon! Hurry! You're gonna *miss_it*!...over *there* where that guy's pullin' out!! (*Mad—snaps*) The *hell* with the guy honkin' behind ya...*just wait*! (*1—2—3—4*) Now!!—pull in! (*Sigh of relief*) Perfect! Great spot! Now we won't have to walk so far. (*Up*) Ron! *Hold it*! Why doncha let the folks out before you pull in all the way...it could be a little...*tight*, for Aunt Marge here. (*Up*) What? I'm not *implying* anything, Marge—I just thought it might be a little...tight! (*1—2—3—4. Sigh of relief*) Well, we're parked anyway. Good spot...(*Annoyed*) Lon! The *trunk*!...open—the—trunk! The luggage, remember? (*Up—quickly*) Now, Ed, don't *you* bother with those bags—Lonnie'll get 'em out! Hands off, now, I mean it!! (*Chuckle*) Till that 'big bird' takes off, you're still on your *vacation*. You gotta remember, Lonnie and I are workin' stiffs...playin' a little hookey from the job! (*Beat*) You get the big ones, will ya, Lon? (*Irritated—quick*) Lon!! The *big ones*! Yeh, *those*. (*Chuckle*) I'll struggle with Aunt Marge's cosmetic case. I'm still savin' up for that hernia operation...O.K. let's go. (*1—2—3—4*) That counter's open, Lon—put 'em down over there. Uncle Ed can get 'em weighed in. (*1—2—3—4. Looks around*) Sure are lots of people here today. You should have good flying weather, the way it looks from *this end*, anyway!! (*Chuckle. 1—2—3—4*) Next, we gotta go through the 'check-point.' I'll put your case on the belt. Marge. (*1—2—3*) *We made it, gang*! Y'see, the thing you don't wanna do, Ed...is look 'suspicious!'... now let's get on the moving sidewalk, or whatever they call it. After you, Marge. (*Beat*) Like I say, just don't look 'suspicious'...but you got nothin' to hide, Ed...(*Sotto*) Now that Margie found your little 'black book!' (*Chuckle*) (*Up*) I'm just kiddin', Marge! For cryin'-out-loud, I was just kiddin' about the 'little black' book!! (*Chuckle—1—2—3*) Ya know, Ed, I didn't *realize*, until we took a chance and *snuck over* *there* yesterday, that the 'Massage Parlor' took MASTER CHARGE! (*Beat—quick*) They oughta call it… 'MISTRESS CHARGE!' (*Chuckle—stops suddenly*) Just kiddin' *again*, Marge! (*Hums lightly*) Actually, we hadda pay *cash*!! (*Beat*) Margie, look at my *face*…do I look as If I'm tellin' the *truth*? I just like to kid around, that's all. (*New thought*) Let's see now…the first thing you'll do is have your lunch on the plane…and maybe *a few belts*, right, Ed? (*Beat*) Oh, you think Ed oughtta stick to soft-drinks, right? Well, they got those too. (*New thought*) Hey, Marge, you see those phone booths? Well, here's a little fun game I came up with! (*Urges her*) Take these *pennies*! (*Stresses it*) C'mon, *take 'em*!! (*Savors this*) Now, here's what you do…you divvy 'em up in the coin-returns on the phones. (*Patient*) The *point* is *this*! Y'see what happens is *this*…the kids around the airport are bored to death, and they like to stick their fingers into the coin-returns for dimes…and I like to see the expressions on their faces when they come up with…*pennies*! They can't figure it out!! (*Chuckle*) Sound like fun? (*Beat*) You don't wanna *do it*? Well, I don't think it's silly! (*Annoyed*) O.K. then gimme 'em back—*I'll* do it some other time. (*1—2—3*) What're we all standin' around for? Let's sit down a while. (*Beat*) Feels good to sit down. (*New thought*) Yah, I was just thinkin' the same thing, Marge. It is a shame that Veronica couldn't come out to the airport with us, but it was just like I told ya, she had this…uh… this important phone call comin' in from…'somebody'…and she didn't want to take a chance of not being there, so I just couldn't *drag* her…I mean, get her to leave the house. (*Beat*) What do I think? About you and Veronica? I…uh…I think you and…uh…Veronica hit it off pretty…uh, pretty well, there. See, I'd told her all about my famous brother and sister-in-law and she…she just kind of knew…what to…expect. (*Chuckle—1—2—3*) There sure are lots of people out here at the air-port today. Ya know what *I* think? *I* think the Chamber of Commerce sends all these people from Central Casting. It makes L.A. look busy!! (*Chuckle—which fades away. Change*) Whadja say, Ed? Oh come on, now! Forget about that—what's done is done! I mean it, forget about the damn stain! (*1—2—3—4*) It's just too bad it wasn't Liebfraumilch, that's all, (*1—2*) Liebfraumilch, Ed…it's a German wine, Ed. (*1—2*) It's a *white* wine, Ed. Y'see, that would've been better…cuz that *red wine* really spreads fast…makes some kind of a *stain* alright. (*Quick—annoyed*) Ed. Listen to me. It was an accident, so *forget it*! (*1—2*) Huh? Oh, Veronica's had that tablecloth for years. It seems that it belonged to her Great-Great Grandmother. Yeh, you're probably right, Marge…it was some kind of an heir-loom. Before it was *willed* to her by her Grandmother, it used to 'trotted out' on State occasions at the White House. (*Beat*) The White House, Ed. (*Beat*) Where the *president* lives. (*Beat*) Not *this* one, Ed…it was Teddy Roosevelt. (*Sigh*) Incidentally, the embroidered pattern on that tablecloth… (*Up—annoyed*) Yeh! Yeh, that's right, Marge…*the one your cigarette burned…that* embroidery pattern was called the Teddy Roosevelt 'Exquisite.' (*Beat*) Yeh, you're right about that, Ed…there weren't a heck of a lot of 'em made. Mater of fact, only three of Teddy's Cousins got one. Veronica's Great-Great Grandmother was one…and it came down the line…Veronica finally got it. (*1—2—3—4*) Oh God, Marge! Don't start up again about *that*!! Tablecloth and *that* didn't have anything to do with Veronica's staying home!! Like I told you, she was expecting this…uh…important…phone-call and she…(*Up—sharply*) Listen!…if you didn't like Veronica's hair-dresser, you didn't like her, that's all! (*Flat out*) Yeh, yeh, you didn't like the way she fixed your hair and *that's it*! (*Beat*) You *what*?…You and *Ed* thought she made you look like a prostitute!! (*To himself*) Oh, my God! (*Up*) What? (*Beat—flat*) Veronica's gone to that hair-dresser for...about... *ten...years*! (*Quick—mad*)...and Veronica's *not* waiting for any lousy *phone-call either*! (*Up*) *You heard me*!! She locked herself in our room, that's what she did!...and when I get home it'll be like walking into a buzz-saw! (*Deadly—spaced*) And when I said I was *kidding* about the massage-parlor...*I wasn't*! (*Snaps it out*) So live with *that* on your way back to Muncie!! (*Storms out*) C'mon, Lon—let's get the hell out of here. You get the car and drive home...I'm gonna *walk*!!

[In this, you want to convey as much about this man's life as possible. He is very lonely and that should come across in how you approach each line. Also, who is he talking to and why is he telling them this? Try it different ways: as if he is trying to get a date with a beautiful woman, as if you are talking to a perspective landlord, etc.]

YOUNG BACHELOR
(Man)

I don' dig dust. See, I got this room where I'm livin'…an' Mrs. Lacy don' give no cleanin' service. Like, if I want it clean, I clean it, right?…So I clean it….yeh, I wash down the walls, I scrub the floor…I put roach powder all around the base-board…an' I dust. (*Up*) I get this here JOHNSON'S stuff an' spray it on this table I got an' the night-stand, (*Throw away*) it ain' much when it comes to furniture…I mean, it ain' like that table Dinah Shore's old husband built himself an' he uses that same polish stuff! (*Change*) Now Mrs. Lacy…she tells me they're gonna tear down this buildin'…I'll never find no place like the one I got…the low rent and all…(*Change*) This old lady, Mrs. Lacy…who runs the place, she's very nervous an' up-tight in this neighborhood…an' she likes a young guy like me aroun' at night. (*Up*) See, I don' run aroun' much…(who can afford it on what I make?)…an' I'm takin' this accountin' course by mail an' I'm always on the premises…so Mrs. Lacy, she never raised my rent or nothin'…but she does with them swingin' singles…she don' dig no hanky-panky. (*Sigh*) But anyways…way it looks…now I prob'ly gotta go live with my sister and my brother-in-law…and Marsha's a lousy housekeeper. (*Pause*) Y'know, I been thinkin'…maybe if I was to pay Marsha a little extra…she'd lemme keep my own room clean…'cause, like I told ya, I don't dig dust!

[This person is not too bright and takes the screenplay very seriously. This is an example of a piece that should be played earnestly. The lines are already funny. No need to punch up the jokes. However, this is another opportunity to use Daws' "fast against slow," "loud against soft" change of pace and dynamics.]

EAR-BENDING AT NATE'N'ALS
(TENNYSON)
(Man or Woman)

...uh...excuse me, Mister Vindonacrill...uh...can...I sit down a minute? uh...thanks...yeh...(*Sits*) I got somethin' I wanna tell ya about...uh...you could be interested, (*Beat*) now listen...this screenplay I got is called TENNYSON. See, Tennyson is this poet, and he lives in this little town, called (*Beat*) I'll hafta get that from research...(*Up*) anyway, this girl...she has this *live dog* named Raoul...an' what Tennyson does, he buys an umbrella from the old umbrella-man down at the corner...(*Up*) I mean, *he's* not old but the umbrellas are. So what happens, this girl steals the umbrella as soon as it starts to rain...and Tennyson gets soaking wet...and Raoul does too...and also a small duck named Olivier with a heart-condition...and Tennyson isn't about to have any of that, so he yells at the girl, 'You stole my umbrella...and certain hardships are being visited on me, Raoul...a *live dog*...and Olivier, a small duck with a heart-condition.' So, the girl, undismayed...but with a blouse that could stand lettin' out...skips back, whacks Tennyson on the head, with the umbrella, snarls at Raoul who was about to do the same thing, but is now intimidated...cuddles the duck a little and resumes her life in a Tibetan monastery...(*Wraps it up*) Well, Tennyson went on to become this famous poet...and the duck got out of show-business entirely. (*Beat*) Huh? Raoul? Oh yeh, well...uh...Raoul, the *live dog*, flipped out when he realized he was under constant contemplation by a patient taxidermist. (*Beat*) Well, whatta ya think Mr. Vindonacrill? I think I got a real winner here, huh?

[You are telling a story that everyone has heard many times so the trick is to say it as if no one has ever heard it before and speak as if you take every word very seriously.]

MARY HAD A LITTLE LAMB
(Man or Woman)

Hey, ya wanna hear a sad story?…lachrymose, even? (That's a cinnamon…means the same thing, you dig?) This story is about this kid…a lil gal an' her name was Mary which is a grand ole name…an'…uh…she had this little lamb whose fleece was white as snow (*Change of pace*) 'course, she woulda preferred havin' a pet like a Boxer, 'cause, you know, in Beverly Hills and…uh…Bel Aire (where them rich dudes live) they pot Boxers and…uh…Dalmatians, an'…uh…them type dogs make a prestige-type pet…(*Change*) But this Mary I was tellin' you about…her old man…he couldn't afford no Boxer or Dalmatian or…uh…none of them type canines, so what he did…he got Mary this here lousy lamb for a pet…'cause, let's face it, he dint have no money comin' in regular, you dig?…Tell ya the truth, he was on welfare, t'tell ya the truth. (*Up*) See, I figger I should oughta tell ya the truth, so I will. Actually, he was doin' time in Alcatraz for lamb-rustlin'…At first, Mary wasn't too overjoyed with her pet lamb…in fact, she was savin' her little pennies for a jar of mint jelly, but her skateboard was broke, and she was too fat to use her hula-hoop (which is some kind of fat if you let your mind dwell on it)…so she accepted the lamb reluctantly, with three month options to terminate the relationship. Anyways, this lamb, who shall be nameless (because I forgot it) was scared alla time, 'cause, y'see, there was this here diploma factory what made sheep skins for graduations, you dig?…an' they had their eye on Mary's lamb,—'cause his fleece was white as snow (you see the way the continuity's goin'?) Well, this lamb, he allus followed Mary around, wherever she went…'cause he figgered the minute he was alone, these diploma guys'd grab 'im! The lamb followed Mary to school, one day, which happened to be against the rule…and not only that, it made the children (not overly bright, but not old enough for the shrink, y'know?) laugh with glee to see a lamb in school…so the teacher told the lamb to 'lam.' (*Beat*) She had a very primitive sense of humor and the children did not laugh with glee at her riposte. So the lamb, lammed and the minute he was outside the school, these guys from the diploma factory, they grab 'im!! An' Mary never seen her lamb again. Well…uh…actually, she did see him one more time…it was when she graduated an' they handed her a sheep-skin what was white as snow. (*Beat*) Didn't I tell ya it was lachrymose?

[This monologue is both a tutorial on the Indian dialect and an exercise in comic timing. The lines should be played to an audience and delivered with a bit of a smile, a joy in the voice. To inflect the Indian sound, place your tongue on the roof of your mouth while speaking.]

INDIAN "STAND-UP" COMIC
(Man)

Ah, tenk you very much…I am very glod to hev de obbortunity of comin' 'ere—you see, ven I talk…like de Indian…it is imbossible…imbossible for me to say imbossible…because I cannot say 'p'…and hard for me to say 't'…so I mus' explain dose barticular vords…dat are very difficult for me to say, y'understand? Because oddervise, you don't know vot I'm talkin' about. (*Change*) Ve hev a lod of people in India…and indeed, in Pakistan…who are loveen to listen to da stand-up comedians…and I vanna tell you dot someday, I vould love to go to Los Angeles…an' go to da comedy-store…and tell some of my jokes…in de United States…Oh, yes indeed! Dat is a gret ambition of mine. Vould you like to hear…jus' a little bit of my routine? I get gret loffs…in India…ven I tell my jokes…beople find it very difficult to maintain their composure, ven I say dees funny things…led me give you an exampul…'ere ve go! Ven Indian men, you know, are tiny babies…dey vear diapers…an ven dey grow up, dey still vear diapers…but dey call it a 'dhoti'…I'm vearing a 'dhoti' right now, an' dat is vot I vear—I forget at dis very moment what da women vear…sari, about dat! (*Up*) Dat's a pun-jab! (*Short laugh*) I go on—I tell more jokes…an' ven ve vere talkin' about diapers, dat remind me dat ven my children vere very small…ve would get my good friend Ravi Shankar to come over and entertain my children…ven dey vere goin' to sleep—we call him a 'baby sitar!' (*Up*) Oh, dat's a very funn…(*Take*) You know, the ladies…in India…dey vear, over dere face…below de eyes, a veil (all de time dey vear a veil)…only you can see dere eyes…an ven dere's a beauty-contest, an' dey take a vote…on da ladies…an' who is the mos' beautiful…de eyes hev it! (*Throw-away*) Dat's a kind of a…small, pun-jab. (*Change*) Ven I vent to da University of Kashmir…vas a gret advancement…my parents vere…very, very delighted…because in our caste, no one hed ever gone to da University of Kashmir…and…and I hed to sweat it out…I…I vas known as the 'Kashmir…(*Take*) Never mind about dat. (*Up*) Lader on, I vas able to go…also to anudder University…da University of Bengal…vere I vas a tiger. I vas as busy…lemme tell you how busy I vas…I vas as busy as a mongoose at a cobra rally. (*Almost breaks up*) Sometimes I find it difficult to maintain <u>my</u> composure (*Giggles—recovers*) but…but I…(*Clears throat*) but I studied very hard…an' I learned a lod of things about India…an' about our vay of thinking and our vay of life…an' our religion…vich is very imbortant for an Indian…or

Pakistan…(Oh, my yes…yes, indeed) for instance, in our religion…ve believe dat some-time ven ve hev left dis vorld…'ve hev left *dis_vorld'*…an' gone into anudder vorld…sometime ve return…ve come back 'ere…vere ve vere before…vere ve lived…da same familiar beople…da same familiar streets…an' I told all my friends…I say, 'ven I die, I vill come back an' you vill know who I am — I vill vear a 'reincarnation!' (*Laugh*) Dat is vot I call a *big* pun-jab! (*Chuckle*) Dat biggest joke in my act…everybody… everybody ask me to repeat dat!…but now it is dime for me to bartake of a little lunch…an' today I am going to try a brand-new blace…it is called (*Beat*) 'da New Delhi!' (*Chuckles*) Vell, anyvay, dat is my act…an' I hope dat you vere able to maintain your composure (*Chuckle*) but not too much!

*[This should be played directly to the audience and as cartoony as
possible. The trick is to have as much fun as possible while still making
this unlikely kid's show host believable.]*

THE UNCLE LEFTY KIDDY SHOW
(1 Man)

LEFTY: Hello, out dere!

Hello, out dere!

Da Uncle Lefty Club welcomes youse!

Now wit the Jolly Burglar,

Please take dis pledge for kicks:

"I will not smoke cigars at all

Til I am almost six!"

Hello, out dere!

Hello, out dere!

Da Uncle Lefty Club welcomes youse!

(*Laughs*) Am I jolly? Am I jolly? Am I comin' through lovable?
Whatta ya say, kids! Dis is yer ole Uncle Lefty again—the friendly
neighborhood burglar. (*Change*) Hey, I wanna read ya a letter I got
from a lil kid in the audience, named Raoul. Raoul says: Dear
Uncle Lefty—instead of jus' tellin' us one story every night—I
would like you to tell two stories. (*Up*) Well, I'll think about it,
Raoul, and congratulations! Yer gettin' to be a reg'lar second story
man!! (*Laughs*) Am I jolly? Am I jolly? Am I comin' through
loveable? (*Up*) But now comes time for the big Uncle Lefty
Contest. But first, fer da benefit of dose kids what was doin' "time"
in the kitchen last night—washin' dishes—I will repeat a few of da
great prizes. Firs' prize—five pairs of Uncle Lefty's gen-u-ine
"finger-print-proof" gloves—dis is a prize yes kin really use, kids—
I mean, why leave incriminatin' fingerprints aroun' da cookie-jar?
(*Laughs*) Whatta ya, wanna be da firs' kid in yer neighborhood wit
a record? An' I don' mean "The Rollin' stones." (*Chuckles*) Shape

up, kids—wear da gloves!! Fer second prize, ya get yer own personal blow-torch—dis one ain't workin' right now. I was gonna get some kerosene fer it on my way to the studio— but unfortunately—the store was open! (*Laughs*) Am I jolly? Am I jolly? Am I comin' through loveable? (*Lowers voice*) Now—I'm gonna tell ya how ya kin win all dese great prizes. (*Lower*) Come in real close to the TV set, kids—dat's right, real close—closer. Now dis is strictly between you an' me, ole loveable Uncle Lefty—it's got nothin' to do wit yer folks. (*Beat*) Now here's what you do. (*Stage whisper*) Draw a pitcher of yer house floor-plan—put an "X" where yer ma keeps the silverware—and if yer old man's got a wall-safe, draw a great big great "X." (I mean, no sense wastin' time on the small stuff, right?) And then send the floor plan in to Uncle Lefty! Simple? Nothing to it! (*Laughs*) Am I jolly? Am I jolly? Am I comin' through lovable?

SOUND: SIREN BUILDING IN INTENSITY

Oh! Oh! Sounds like company! The fuzz! I gotta cut out!! Now, remember, kids—keep a blow-torch in the winda fer yer ole Uncle Lefty!

SOUND: SIREN FULL UP—THEN OUT WITH BRAKE SCREECH

(*Fading*) An' don' fergit!—Wear da gloves!!!

[The key to this philosophical monologue is to decide who are you talking to, where are you and why you are telling this. It is as much about listening to the reaction of the imagery person you are talking to as how you say the lines themselves. Does the person want to hear what you are saying? Are you saying it to be helpful or mean? Try it several ways.]

LIFE IS EATING A LOBSTER
(Male or Female)

(*Note: eliminate the section within [ ] if you are a woman*)

I think of life as eating a lobster. I mean, so much of it doesn't matter—the good part is in the claws and the tail. (*Up*) What're you laughing at? I'm serious! Most of it you throw away. I live inside…aware of and most of the time pretty content with the experiences I know I'll never to be able to share—and probably don't want to share. That are private—that're mine. With someone who matters—with you—I'll always have plenty to share…but you've gotta realize there's those undefinables—those imponderables—the margins for error or success—but they're mine. And you've got yours too—and what you don't want me to know I don't wanna know. (*Change*) The inside—that's the important part—that sweetness held in the claws—and it doesn't come easy—you've gotta know how to get at it. I don't pay a hell of a lot of attention to externals—to the way I dress (which I guess you could also call sloppy)…I try to keep my table manners from being completely barbaric…I live inside. I see, inside 'you' what I want to see—what's mine to see—what you allow me to see. The rest of 'em, the clods—the ones who always tie their laces and keep trying to find a cure for dandruff—those questionable creatures…'they' can see the 'outside' of you…I mean, what's on the counter, by the cash-register for an impulsive sale…that isn't the 'you' I want…the 'you' that I know is all mine. Try to fight back a laugh, but it's my only conceit. I mean it! (*Change*) To me, the inside of my house is the best part—the only part that matters to me—my office, where I write—where I see those precious little black marks pop out on the paper…where my books are stacked…the trash mixed in with the classics because all books are good. My memorabilia—the things I love. (*Change*) The outside of the house (my eyes pretend not to see the peeling paint) I try to keep just presentable enough so the joggers won't cluck their tongues and shake their heads as they perform their dismal, daily Calvary. See, I'm really not all that interested in the 'outside' of anything—it's the part of the lobster I can discard. (*Change*) If you live inside—deep inside—you don't see entities or things aging…they stay the same except for their enhanced growth—they're constantly being honed, polished. See, I think of my mind as a womb and my thoughts, my desires and my ideas can be born—and reborn—many times…and they're not 'clones,' those ideas—they're all different. As I grow, they grow. (*Warms to it even more*) I live in sweaters, an old car that is only an expedient…I eat simple food—and I relate to you. (*Softly*) How important the whole schmear would be without you, I donno. I only barely accept such a notion, but I didn't always have you—but I have you now and the temperature of my contentment doesn't vary. (*Change*) Living inside—knowing the meat of two claws—is enough for me. (*New thought*) Funny, when I smoked—I thought I was enjoying the taste (the smoke spiraling up)…the taste. [There was something dramatic about packing a pipe-bowl…and then the first sucking in of the lighted tobacco…and I truly believed the taste to be enjoyable. I guess I did, somewhat…I thought I should…it was a part of the pipe-smoker's commitment]—but it wasn't until I stopped smoking completely that I realized that my olfactory sense was enjoying tremendously the aroma of 'someone else' smoking! I found the aroma delicious—so you see, my thesis is this. It's got to be one or the other—joining the pack and thinking that you're enjoying life…or to be 'with them' but not 'of them'…to back off and discover that staying on the rim of the circle and observing what's inside is even more fulfilling! To keep growing…with negotiable commitments…to be like a river, turning over. To not get stagnant…to experience many births…to keep breaking the mold that first held you—to rebuild and save what you can from the old sinews! The elastic must never harden—the stretching must be constant! Life, as I said, can be likened to the edible part of the lobster. There isn't much that can be uniquely yours—but it is your commitment to find it…and with it, fulfillment. Fulfillment is the target—that's what you're going for. Throw the rest of it away.

[The challenge here is to evoke a frightening sense of power and a pitying feeling of loneliness at the same time.]

LOVE THE WORTHY
(Male or Female)

Face forward!…you may look at me. (*Beat*) I love you all…and I have found you worthy of my love. This was not always so, but it is…now. The people whom I attract (and will continue to attract) or who are attracted to me…are all splendid types! Exemplary! In my entourage, there are no zealots, idealists, humanists. (*Up*) No laughter, please!…No self-centered aggressors, no one of strong-will, no questioners…no dreamers of a dream. (*Up—sharp*) I *said*: no laughter! The people with whom I have surrounded myself are tractable…they follow my line of reasoning—exactly. They accept, without question, my concepts (as well they should…my background verifies my credo!)…and they do all that must be done…in my way…and my way only! My credibility must be a sacred thing… always. (*Chuckle—lightly*) Oh, many's the time I've chuckled over the tears…frustrations and 'hurt' expressions on the faces of those 'weaklings' who couldn't…or wouldn't accept the inevitability of their…'personality loss.' (*Up*) No laughter! (*Grim*) I warn you…there will be punishment!…and yet, in the golden, astral sense…it's not a loss at all…there is no loss. There *is* an alternative…what they would have in its stead, would be a straight-forward, knowledgeable…and undeviating point-of-view. No dark corners. No closets. No self-doubts (because there would be little of 'self' left, am I not right?) (*Up*) Please! Eye-acknowledgment only!…no…audible… expression!…we go on. Their minds, replete with a fully programmed and controlled intelligence…would, with a reverse sponge-action…purge the garbage-memorabilia of their past fractional life…leaving only…for immediate use (an any time!) the super-computerized-wisdom which I have instilled in them…which I have entrusted them *with* (*Strong*) for their worthiness must be valid at all times!…I, as you could never know, having lost your expendable memory… (but will now because I tell you)…brook no opposition! I accept no questions. They desire my knowledge. They surrender their independence to achieve it. When it is instilled in them…they cease to exist. (*Finality*) They are me…they are all 'me.' 'You' are 'me!' The misfits I eliminate…and have eliminated…and will continue to eliminate!…and this…has ennobled me…and given me the purity to 'love the worthy'…who have given me their souls!

[How do you make a boring speech interesting? Not every line an actor reads will be great. You must find the ways to make it interesting.]

TO TELL IT LIKE IT IS, OR NOT TO TELL IT LIKE IT IS
(1 Man or Woman)
(with apologies to William Whats-his-name)...but NOT Howard!!!

To tell it like it is, or not to tell it like it is—a rather succinct way of expressing what is—at its base—a ponderous philosophical evaluation of one's destiny. There is a pro-pensity -governed by one's cerebral power—to put up with—or 'bite the bullet,' if you will—to prepare one's self for the ammunition sent one's way by an ubiquitous presence...on the other hand, should one put on the brass-knucks and go after this great mass of bad news?—And with the proverbial 'chip on one's shoulder'—bring the matter to a satisfactory conclusion? (*Pause*) To cash in one's chips—to hit the sack...fade out, cut and print and hope for a tax loss—and may I add—no re-runs or even syndication interest. (*Beat*)...and by grabbing a bit of sack-time, we put the kibosh on a bunch of possible contenders who could bloody our noses! (*Lays it out*) Because it was so written in the record book. (*Beat*) This is a matter that we can't dismiss too readily...tis an end-all we should go for. (*Pause*) To cash in one's chips (as I mentioned earlier)—to snooze—perhaps to experience some beddy-bye vagaries. (*Up*) Now that's where you'll find your-self in big trouble—for in that nap that isn't going to have any ham and eggs waiting in the morning, because of the fact that we'll be putting in a bit of 'harp-time' in the non-union universe, makes us reflect for a moment...that's why it's a bad scene if we stick around the old neighborhood too long. (*Dramatic*) For who is going to put up with the kidney punches and smart-aleck remarks of longevity. (*Long pause—clears throat*) There's a lot more to this—but I'm going to call a halt and there's a reason. I'm beginning to bore *myself!*

[This is the female version of "A Bad Time was had by All." Again, the parenthetical directions should be played exactly as written, except for the ones marked (Change) *which are open to interpretation. Why is this woman rambling? Is she egotistical, insecure, nervous, drunk? Try it as many ways as you can think of.]*

DONNA
(Woman)

(*Calls*) Ed! Ed Brown!! Over here! (*Beat*) Ed! Gosh, it's not *'fancy* meeting you here'…in this dump. I mean, you, the gourmet…with a tray in your hand yet! (*Beat*) Siddown! (*Up*) Oh, Ed! Gosh, it's good to see ya! (*Up*) I'm gonna put my tray'n'stuff on this next table…make our table look classier! (*Giggles*) D'you remember the time you took me to Perinos and got mad cuz I didn't dig it? (*Pause—throw-away*) You don't remember? Well, then, maybe I dreamt it…what did I know from Perinos? (*Change*) Where've you been, Ed? You just dropped out of sight…(*Up*) Canada? You shot the picture in Canada? Well, Ed, why didn't you let me know…I was goin' crazy there! (*Change*)…and what're you doin' in *this* neighborhood (*Beat*) You're kiddin'…you called my answering service and they told you I was here! (*Throw-away*) Well, why not…I always leave locations, even when I go to the bathroom! See, I gotta play percentages…I might lose a job…or a chance to go to the ball. (*Up*) A chance to meet PRINCE AD-EQUATE!! (*Looks around*) This place…this place is 'barely' a location, (*Up*) it's certainly not a decent cafeteria…(*Up*) It's not even as good as PERINOS (and you know what I think about PERINOS!!) Oh, God! I'm rambling!!! I get this way sometimes! (*Change*) What am *I* doing here? I hadda take my car next door for service. (*Up*) Sure, it's a lousy neighborhood, but you gotta understand, Ed—in this neighborhood, I get work done cheaper. It's economics…pure and simple…I just add mugging to collision and comprehensive!! (*Laughs*) Hey. I just noticed…Ed! What're you eating? You are…eating…stuffed bell-peppers!! Yukkk! Come *onnnnn*, Ed—nobody eats stuffed bell-peppers in a joint like this!! (*Giggles*) No! wait a minute…it's okay for you! You know why? Cuz I remember one of your 'quotables…' (*Clears throat*)…'If I can stomach Actors…I can stomach ANYTHING! (*Change*) NO, Ed…really…I don't want anything else. I'm fine!…unless I could promote a Charlotte Russe. (*Up*) Charlotte Russe, Ed…it's sort of a lady-finger dessert…with gobs of whipped cream…I mean, real whipped cream!!…not, that *out of the can*…whipped cream…real whipped cream!! A Charlotte Russe! Nobody knows what I'm talkin' about. Do you, Ed?…Nobody knows! (*Pause*) My mom used to make 'em when I was a kid. The Charlotte Russe was very popular then… with her, anyway. What it is, a Charlotte Russe is sort of a lady-finger dessert…with gobs of whipped cream and a cherry on top…easy t'make, y'know…an' my mom dug 'easy'… cuz she wasn't home all that much…(*Change*) What'm I talkin' about? I'm goin' on and on about a dumb ole Charlotte Russe…and what I really wanna do, is talk about you, Ed!! (*Pause*) You!!! It's so good to see you…I missed you. (*Change*) When'd you get back from Canada? You flew in today! (*Up*) Today!! I'm a welcoming committee!!! (*Suddenly serious*) Ed…I was goin' crazy…wonderin' what happened. You said you wanted me for Clara, Ed. I got three call backs and you said I was terrific and you'd call me for sure that Monday…that long ago 'what the hell ever happened to that Monday?' (*Softly*) My God, how long's it been? Couple months? (*Up*) Please…don't look like that, Ed…I'm just tellin' you what it was like. (*Sigh*) You said, 'Donna, looks like we finally got us a deal! I slanted a part and it reads like you!' (*Up*) I was so excited, Ed!! You used to say 'Don't get excited…let it happen.' (*Softly*) I wanted to be so good for you, Ed. (*Pause*) I waited out that terrible Monday…never left the apartment…I waited. Even at night, I went to bed about one…watched Carson for a while…then I called my answering service. (*Imitates operator*) 'All clear!!' (They love to say that!!) (*Up*) No…wait, Ed. You can talk later on…I been savin' up! (*Change*) You wanna know what hurt the most? You know what destroys me when I think of it…'cause it was so 'special?'…You…you cupped my chin with your hand the way you do…and you called me 'Kid'…you said 'kid, you're gonna make it!' (*Pause*) Tell me, Ed. Who finally played Clara?…Maggie? (*Up*) Oh God, not Maggie! You said yourself, Ed…you said she wasn't young enough or good enough to get away with it anymore. (*Pause—softly*) Why Maggie, Ed? You said you slanted the part for me. (*Up*) Hennessey wanted Maggie? The 'big' producer wanted her? (*Beat*) Sure, I'm mad! Why didn't you fight for me, Ed?…you coulda swung it, I know,—I was so 'right' for Clara. (*Pause*) Well, anyway…you look embarrassed, Ed…and sad. Well. I'm glad you're sad and you're letting me see it. Why didn't you at least call me? Did you think I couldn't take rejection from you? (*Pause—quietly*) You don't really owe me a damned thing, Ed…it's just that you've always been so special to me. You were just there when I needed someone like you. You talked to me. You made me aware of myself as a person long before I was the kind of an actress I'd have to be for you to use me. You used to say 'Stand up to the words…don't let 'em bully you!…They're only dead symbols—they don't mean a thing until you get 'em off the paper and up in your computer—until you spit 'em out new-born as your 'thoughts'…They won't be the writer's anymore—they'll be yours.' (*Softly*) You said that…to me, Ed—and it was a door I needed. (*Change*) You finish your bell peppers? (*Giggles*) You must have. Your face is green! (*Up*) Huh? You wanna go where? You're teasing me! Ed, I haven't the foggiest idea where we could find a Charlotte Russe in this neighborhood! (*Change*) Hey, how about this? Wanna take me to Perino's? (*Flippant*) After all, I am an actress—I'll try to dig it!!

[Try to bring as much subtext as possible to this short monologue. Why is the girl so distraught over a dress? Is she just nervous about the wedding? Is there something else going on in her life she's not talking about? How does her past history with her mother effect her emotionally at this moment?]

EMOTIONAL DISAPPOINTMENT
(Woman)

Mother! (*Beat*) Mother! You listen now, I listened and I'm not having any! I am not going to wear it. I put it on to please you but I will not wear it to the wedding. Don't you remember when Aunt Deedee said she would make the dress and I could pick the color and you know pink is my favorite color. But I know my pink. The pink I like. Mother, it has to be more than pink. This is a dumb pink and I hate it and I will not wear it. Mother, Aunt Deedee wouldn't have gone to all the trouble of making the dress if I wasn't going to like it. I hate it! She told me I could go with her and pick out the pink I wanted and I could have gone—I didn't have to go to that stupid dance class—but you said I was busy and now I've got on a pink dress I hate! (*Up*) Whatta you mean I'll just have to wear it once. (*Quietly furious*) For your information, mother, and if I'm being a smart alec I'm being a smart alec—I am not wearing this dumb dress at all. (*Change*) My cousin Jan can wear it. (*Pause*) O.K. you're right—she's too tall. But she can show off more of her legs and she'd love that! (*Beat*) I am not going to be a part of the wedding at all. I'm not stubborn! (*Beat*) Yes, I am! I'm stubborn and I'm mad and I'm not going to be sweet about it! I hate that "Denise is such a sweet child!" I won't say the word the kids say but I'm thinking it. (*Quiet and close to tears*) Now I'm going to tear off this sickly pink dress. (*Pause—tearful*) I'm...I'm sorry I made you cry, mother. I know there won't be a next time because I've only got one sister, but if there is a next time, let me pick out my own pink!!

[This is an exercise in creating tension by letting the character's frustration slowly build. Do not start at too high an emotional level or you will have no where to go. Use the BEATS to bring you to the next level. Imagine what Fred is doing while you are talking.]

FRED AND TRUDY MONOLOGUE
(1 Woman)

Fred! Start the car! (*Beat*) I am *sitting* in the *back seat*—so start the car and let's get this over with! (*Beat*) I don't *want* to sit in the front seat. I'm not *going* to sit in the front seat, so *start the car*!! (*Annoyed breath expulsion*) It doesn't make *sense*... *that's* why! We'll just have to change later on, when we pick up Dick and Edna... don't be a child!!—Dick'll sit in front with you like he *always* does... so you can go on and on about your *beloved* Dodgers. (*Beat*) *Start the car.* (*Beat*) The only cute one the Dodgers ever had was that Steve Garvey and they dumped him. Good riddance! (*Beat*) No, pea-brain, *not* Steve Garven, the 'Dodgers!!' Steve doesn't need those bums—and I don't need *Dick* or *Edna* or *you*! This could very well be our last night together, so *grow up*, for God's sake!! You're hung up on patterns—*puberty* patterns! (*Beat*) The first time you *made out* with me was in a car—the back-seat was your security blanket. You never grew up... you just wanna relive your little conquest over-and-over. You want me in the front seat *now*, but after we leave Dick and Edna—your panting little psyche has got great plans for the back-seat!!! It took you weeks to get up the *nerve* for your big *romance*... and you never got over it... you've gotta keep reliving it... over and over... and *over*! (*Beat*) *Get it through your head, Buster*!... I am... *leaving you* tomorrow... (*Firm*) All my things are at my mother's! (*Up*) *Tonight*, if you'll start this damned car, we're gonna pick up your *beloved* Dick and Edna and... (*Snaps*) Well, they're *certainly* not *my* 'beloved' Dick and Edna! I'll be getting *them* outta my hair, too! *Fringe benefits*!! All she ever does is watch soap-operas, to bone up on her 'sex technique'—and lust after Dick between innings, for God's sake!! We're going out to dinner tonight, because those stupid reservations finally came through—*three months* we waited!! Just because you and your *beloved* Dodger freak had this damn *thing* about Basque food, for God's sake! (*Spits it*) *Basque!*—maybe that's what you oughta do, go out and live with the sheep for awhile—you're not up to their intelligence but you could get a great harem, made to order! (*Up—mad*) *Start the car, dammit!* I wanna get this night, the hell over with!! I am looking forward to our separation. (*Pause*) What? (*Beat*) Oh, I guess I didn't bother to tell you. Mother and I are finally getting around to cataloguing the pewter collection. (*Beat*) Start the *car!! Will you start the damned car!* (*Beat*) I don't *know* how long it'll take... there's quite a lot of pewter, probably several weeks. (*Up—annoyed*) The separation? How the hell do I know how long it'll take! Start this car... and I mean *now*!

[This character comes on at full energy. The challenge is to keep this going throughout by pulling back, pausing, sighing, thinking (etc.) before saying a line, saying a line to yourself, reacting to others around you, and all the while slightly yelling over the crowd at the Los Angeles airport.]

GLENHALL AND BETTS
(Woman)

Sorry it took so long to park, Betts…this airport was obsolete before it was finished…it's a mess. Look, I wanna get some cigarettes…just take a second. (*Up*) Why don't you sit down and wait for the boys…Herman gets panicky if I'm not where he expects me to be at the airport. (*Beat*) No, he doesn't worry about me exactly…he just has this thing about airports…I mean, he hates airports. When there's no way out, he goes to 'em, does what you're supposed to do at an airport…and gets his little butt out as fast as he can. Ha likes to know where I am all the time so I don't slow him down— the only time-table he's got is in his mundane mind! (*Sigh*) Herman is an intense C.P.A. and his avocation is doing over old houses…that's his life, prescribed and private, never being with more than a couple people at one time. Airports to him are rowdy and blatant…they make him uncomfortable. To him, there's an obscene voraciousness in the way they gobble up people and spew them out…what he calls 'the grubbies'…with the string-tied bundles and the shopping bags. Herman could very easily become a snob! Airports make him aware of another world out there. He isn't interested…*at all*…in 'that' world. He would like to put 'that world' on microfilm…file it…and never refer to it again! (*Up*) Are you kidding? No, he doesn't…he doesn't like any part of 'people watching.' (*Thinks*) Well, I suppose he wouldn't mind glomming a little leg crossing…but what with all the pants and slack-suits these days, his C.P.A. mind gives up on the percentages! (*Up*) So, why don't you sit down and wait for the boys…and I'll go and get my cigarettes.

Yeh, my cigarettes and a season ticket to Murder Anonymous! We have three racing meets out here every year…and Glenhall and Betts hafta make 'em all…on us!! On our time and hospitality! Three times a year we've got houseguests…but they're the same boring ones!! The same conversation! Horse-talk…horse-talk!!…and the man with the broom and shovel *follows* horses for what 'they' talk about!! (*Sigh*)…and the same old dirty jokes…they're so gross!…and *Glenhall* tells a few goodies himself! Of course, my Herman thinks it's so cute when Betts goes Anglo-Saxon…which is most of the time with that little angel-face! The 'private parts' of speech, for God's sake!! (*Up*) Oh, Miss…cigarettes, please! (Beat) What? Oh any kind…doesn't matter. I mean, I hate this damned habit and I'll be damned if I'll cater to its preferences!!…gimme anything! (*Up*) Except filtered! (*Giggles*) I gotta draw the line somewhere!!…thanks!

Well! I see you boys got the bags on O.K…you got stuff to carry on the plane with you? Well, sure, the Racing Form I figured…but what else? A new book?…this it?…lemme see! (*Up*) Oh, this is wild…take a look at this, Herman!…come on, you guys, you're not serious! I can see it printed on the dust-jacket, but…(*Giggles*)…the Horse Horoscope!! That's for real? Astrology for horses? You mean, you believe that stuff? Well, sure…it *could* be a whole new system, but you know what I think? I think the guy who wrote all this guff is gonna make a lot more money from horse-lovers like you two…than you are on the 'system!' (*Bridles*) I am *not* up-tight about it and I am *not* making a 'thing' out of it…I just turn off on some of the way-out stuff that turns you guys on, that's all! (*Change*)…and besides, we don't dig horses all that much, do we, Herman? You and Glenhall think the sport of kings is great because it gives you a strong 'mutual' interest…sorry about that!…but Herman and I get our kicks with the sport of 'queens'… interior decorating…right, Herman? Remember those places we pointed out when we were driving around? Well, Herman and I…we did those places over—now they look like *something*! We couldn't take you inside to show you what we did but we're a terrific team. Of course, the clods who live in those houses are still clods…we just fix up houses…not clods. I suppose we should feel guilty for over-charging 'em…but whatta clods know? (*Giggle*) What's that, Herman? The bar? (*Aside*) You want a drink, Betts? Glenhall?…well, I don't. Why don't you three go get a drink…I'll come get ya when the boarding call comes…O.K.? (*Up*) No, you go on ahead…I'll be fine!!

Glenhall loves a crowded bar…with standees…women standees, naturally. He likes to bump their fannies when he's fighting for a bar position. I swear I got so sick of his bumping against me…I swear, if I went into that bar this very minute…and he did it again, he'd end up a soprano for the Vienna Boy's Choir…I swear! (*Sigh*) Now all I've gotta do is sit here all by my lonesome and wait for that blessed boarding-call! Poor Glenhall… poor Betts! Maybe it does 'em good being here with me once in a while…maybe some of my honest normalcy will rub off on them.

[Playing "ditsy" and not falling into a stereotype can be one of the most difficult changes for any female actor. Try thinking of what just happened to this character right before she spoke. Try playing the scene as if she is not ditsy but just nervous. Then, play it as if she is ditsy but knows she is.]

YELLOW FLOWERS
(Woman)

I wrote a book about those yellow flowers. (*Pause*) I forget now what you call them…all those yellow flowers look alike to me…jonquils, I guess they were…or daisies. (*Pause*) I have several books in preparation. I'm dedicated to my art…Once, all by myself, I published a book with letters from a real Mattell printing press! I called it 'Red Flowers'…it's all about red flowers. (*Conviction*) I will call it 'Red Flowers'…(*Titters*) That's the working title…I may call it something else later on. (*Pause*) I also have roughed out a book about blue flowers. I'm beating my brains out for a title, but one will come to me, I'm sure. (*New subject*) I did some exploratory research on fudge also…it was sort of an escape valve…and just in time! See, I discovered that my intense concentration on different colored flowers was driving me up the wall…and it soon became apparent to me that a change in my writing regimen was indicated. (*Pause*) Writing has been my whole life…my reason for being…once I wrote a keen article where I spelled some of the words right…but it never got published. It fell on the floor and the dog ate it. See, my father was a baker and I used to write on bread…we couldn't afford paper. (*Up*) Will you excuse me now? Ray Bradbury keeps looking over here. I think he wants his pencil back.

[How do you stop to listen and maintain excitement for what you are saying? This girl's enthusiasm for her story cannot wane in spite of what she hears on the other end of the phone.]

YOUNG MATRON (ON TELEPHONE)
(Woman)

I did! I really did! I mean, what's the point? I should make somethin' like that up? She was. She was in the FOOD KING this morning…an' I was in the FOOD KING this morning, an' I said: 'Oh, my God! It's Vanessa Redgrave!' (*Listens*) It was about six-thirty. (*Listens*) Don't give me that 'they don' open 'til nine o-clock jazz!' – it's open all night! Twenty-four hours. It's open! (*Listens*) Not the one you go to, maybe, but the one I go to, is. (*Lays it out*) There's like four people in the whole store and two of 'em are me and Vanessa Redgrave who looks just the same but I thought she was even *taller*. (*Listens*) Huh? Because I needed baloney for the kid's sandwiches an' I was awake, so I went in my house-coat, I dint even turn on the lights. (*Listens*) Why bother Charlie? He was sleepin' in, cuz they had this meetin' last night that lasted for God knows! So what I did, I picked up the HEBREW NATIONAL. (*Listens—up*) So my kids like it spicy, that's why, and anyway, it's all beef and there's Vanessa Redgrave at the check-stand! (*Listens*) Because she looked like Vanessa Redgrave, that's how!…an', Eloise, listen! When the checker said somethin' to her, she said somethin' back in English. (*Listens*) I mean, 'English' English! (*Listens*) What's hard to believe? You're just green, that's all…I can tell. What about that time you saw the WALTON'S writer, Earl Hamner at McDonald's, eatin' a fruit pie…you coulda been wrong about him, y'know! I mean, who sees Earl Hamner except maybe some old picture in TV GUIDE that was taken ten years ago…but 'she' was on just the other night. She was on TV, Vanessa Redgrave, on the 'late-late,' after Johnny Carson (*Listens*)…with Sean Connery, she fell off her horse an' he finally married her an' I went to bed right after I saw it was her…I saw it before anyway. (*Listens—up*) What difference does it make! (*Listens*) You finally gettin' around to that…she was wearin' this jump suit like a mechanic…looked like nothin' and she could afford whatever. She paid for her stuff an' dint take her green stamps—so I did. (*Listens*) Why not? I figgered if I didn't, the checker would and it's about time we got somethin' back from England anyway. (*Listens*) Yeh, quite a morning. (*Quickly*) Look, I gotta hang up…I hear Charlie an' the kids yellln'. (*Listens*) O.K., come on over, after…but what more can I tell ya…she was wearin' this jump suit. 'Bye!

The Editors

BEN OHMART lives in Boalsburg, Pennsylvania where he runs BearManor Media, a small publishing company dedicated to books on old radio and old films. His current projects include biographies on Paul Frees, Daws Butler, The Bickersons, and Don Ameche.

JOE BEVILACQUA first wrote to Daws Butler when he was 16 years old in 1975. Soon after, Daws appointed himself Joe's personal mentor and thus began a whirlwind 13-year apprenticeship. Bevilacqua has gone on to become a veteran award-winning radio producer, documentarian and dramatist, whose work has been heard on public stations throughout the United States, Canada, the British Isles and Australia. He has created programs for National Public Radio, Public Radio International, Pacifica, XM Satellite Radio, among others. His documentary "Lady Bird Johnson: Legacy of a First Lady" was heard on nearly 200 public radio stations and was the best documentary finalist at the 2001 New York Festivals competition. He has written and produced over 100 radio plays, including the popular comedy radio theater series, "The Misadventures of Sherlock Holmes" and his pet project—an 18-part half-hour surrealistic radio comedy series, "The Whithering of Willoughby and the Professor," in which he performs all the characters himself. Carrying on the tradition of his mentor, Bevilacqua conducts acting workshops in the Catskill Mountains of New York State.

Characters Actor

The official biography of
Daws Butler

by Ben Ohmart and Joe Bevilacqua

Coming Christmas 2004

From BearManor Media

BearManor Media
P O Box 750
Boalsburg, PA 16827
http://bearmanormedia.com

SCENES

for ACTORS and VOICES

by Daws Butler

Edited by

Ben Ohmart *and* Joe Bevilacqua

Daws Butler was the Master of Voice. He spoke the words for most of the classic Hanna-Barbera characters: Yogi Bear, Huckleberry Hound, Quick Draw McGraw, Elroy Jetson, and a hundred others. He also originated the vocal character of Cap'n Crunch and other famous Jay Ward cartoon characters. His significant work as both a writer and an actor with Stan Freberg in the 1950s on *The Stan Freberg Show* and multi-million-selling records such as *St. George and the Dragonet* are still held in reverence today. He also ran a voice acting workshop for years.

This is his book of scenes, exercises and advice for voice actors, written for those who are now tops in the profession. Among his many successful students are Nancy Cartwright (voice of Bart Simpson), and Corey Burton (from *Closet Cases of the Nerd Kind* to Disney's *Treasure Planet*), who wrote the Foreword.

For the first time in print, finally a book for voice professionals by the top man himself!

ISBN: 0-9714570-6-9 $15.95 + $2 US postage to:

Wholesalers welcome.

BearManor Media
P O Box 750, Boalsburg, PA 16827
or order online at http://bearmanormedia.com